SOLVING CRYPTIC CROSSWORDS

How to crack those cryptic clues

B. J. Holmes

BLOOMSBURY

A BLOOMSBURY REFERENCE BOOK

www.bloomsbury.com/reference

First published 2002
as *The Guide to Solving Crosswords*

This second edition published in 2003 by
Bloomsbury Publishing Plc
38 Soho Square
London W1D 3HB

British Library Cataloguing-in-Publication Data

A catalogue record for this book is available from the British Library

ISBN 0-7475-6643-7

Text computer typeset by Bloomsbury Publishing
Printed and bound in Italy by Legoprint

Crossword Clues and Extracts

Throughout this book we have used clues and parts of clues to illustrate a particular
style of puzzle and how to solve the clue. It would have been difficult and confusing to
include the source of each clue in the main layout of the book. Instead, we have
credited the sources below. The clues we have used have come from a range of
newspapers and magazines — we are indebted to the crossword setters for making the
puzzles interesting, challenging and enjoyable to solve!

The publications used as sources include:

*Chicago Tribune, Daily Express, Daily Mail, Daily Mirror, The Daily Record,
Daily Star, Daily Telegraph, Financial Times, The Guardian, Houston Chronicle,
Independent, Independent on Sunday, Irish Independent, The Irish Times,
New York Times, The Observer, Radio Times, The Sun, Sunday Telegraph,
Sunday Times, The Sydney Morning Herald, The Times, The Times of India,
The Toronto Globe and Mail, USA Today.*

Trademarks

All terms mentioned in this book that are known to be registered trademarks or trade
names have been capitalised. Bloomsbury Plc is not associated with any product or
vendor mentioned in this book and cannot guarantee the accuracy of this trademark or
trade name information.

PREFACE

It is said that the world is divided into two kinds of people: those who like dividing everybody into two groups — and those who don't. Laying aside the cynicism of that observation, the world *is* certainly divided into those who enjoy doing cryptic crosswords and those for whom they are unfathomable. The former category included the late and great Sir John Gielgud, along with Richard Burton who had the proviso written into his contract that he be allowed to tackle the cryptic puzzle in his morning paper before being called to the set. Kill-joys are exemplified by the well-known journalist who was heard by the writer (while actually writing these words) to proclaim sneeringly that life is too short for bothering with crosswords. Revealingly, he added that they posed an impenetrable barrier to him anyway. He's right in one respect. To the casual observer or beginner, cryptic clues use a language that certainly looks like English; but there the similarity seems to end.

However, for those who wish to share in the enjoyment of cryptic crosswords there is a basic key to understanding them. Once that is realised, the door is open. We are not saying that from then on solutions will come easy. If they were easy, there wouldn't be a challenge — and the challenge that they pose is the essence of the enjoyment.

The secret is simply this: the reason why the clues read like gobbledygook is that in most clues their compiler is using **code**, two sets of codes in fact. One set of codes represents **building blocks** (words, part-words and abbreviations) to build up answers. And the second set of codes represents the **operations** that one is required to do with the building blocks. In the remaining clues that don't quite fit this pattern, the compiler is either using conventions or just having fun with words. Moreover, in many cases the 'answer' part of a clue lies at either the beginning or end of the clue. Once you become familiar with these practices — and that's the purpose of this book — then you are well on the way to solving and successfully completing whole grids on your own.

In the captivating film *Mrs Muncke* an old man played by Bruce Dern is mulling over a crossword and comes out with the statement 'No matter how many of these darn things I try I always end up feeling a fool!' At the moment, you may know what he means. But by the time you get to the end of this book you're going to have far less reason to share the unfortunate Mr Dern's feelings.

Acknowledgements

I would like to thank Dave Eades for working through the manuscript and for his valuable suggestions. Any remaining mistakes are my own.

B.J. Holmes

CONTENTS

INTRODUCTION

Before we get going and before you turn the page, have a stab at solving this clue.

Popular sounding ghost has the code to give policeman on TV (9,5)

	1			2		3		4			4		2

If you haven't 'got a clue' after considering it as it stands for a while, look below for some help, *still without turning the page*.

1. When you are tackling clues in an actual crossword it is possible you will already have a letter or two in place. So, throughout the book, if and when you are stuck with one of our practice clues, you will have the option of putting in some letters (keyed with numbers) which will be offered in a table at the end of the relevant section. For example, the letters at the bottom of this page may help you with the above clue. To get the most value out of our exercises it is recommended that, rather than put in all the letters in one go, you put each letter in singly, then have another think at the answer before inserting a further letter.

2. At the end of the book you will find a glossary, which has been especially prepared to help you with all our practice clues. Feel free to refer to it at any time — starting now. So if you are still stuck after putting in the four 'free' letters, look up each of the clue's words in turn.

1	2	3	4
N	E	T	R

The answer is INSPECTOR MORSE — but if you didn't crack it, don't be put off. That kind of clue, and indeed ones more difficult, is the kind of clue that you should be able to solve by the end of this book. As we are still at the very beginning of things, we are not immediately concerned with how the answer to that particular clue was arrived at — but if you are eager at this early stage to get involved in the intricacies, see below[1].

Inspector Morse, TV's late lamented detective, is a good starting point for our own investigations because he was a *cruciverbalist*, a fancy term someone once dreamt up meaning an enthusiast for crossword puzzles. Along with his red Jaguar and penchant for best bitter, this quirk added to Morse's character but at the same time his creator Colin Dexter was making a point. The ability to solve cryptic crosswords requires an ability not unlike that required to solve murder mysteries. The classic English whodunit, in its form laid down by Agatha Christie, is a game between the murderer and detective, where the villain will lay down false clues which the intrepid investigator is required to recognise and side-step. Similarly, the solver of a cryptic crossword needs to identify the compiler's attempts to lead him or her up the garden path.

When the government was recruiting personnel to crack German codes during the Second World War, one of the qualifications for consideration to be on the team was an interest in, and ability to solve, cryptic crosswords. The idea behind this was that the hallmark of the cryptic puzzle is the deliberate laying of traps to get the solver to fall for the obvious. And candidates whose brains where already practiced in avoiding the obvious, albeit in innocuous crossword puzzles, were more likely to prove useful in the serious business of cracking enemy codes.

Incidentally, while it seems that compilers are mainly male, the solving of crosswords is enjoyed equally by women and men.

Edward de Bono, the popular psychologist, argued that there are two kinds of thinking. Firstly, there is the everyday kind — straightforward logic that proceeds step by step. Then there is what he called **lateral thinking**, where one sidesteps obvious logic to come up with something unexpected. Of course, straightforward logic is necessary for us to get by and tackle most of the problems that life puts our way. However, another way to describe following a straight logical progression is being in a rut. Lateral thinking — going sideways — gets your mind out of the rut, helps you to avoid the obvious.

As the puzzle compiler uses lateral thinking when constructing his cryptic clue, so must you and I as the solvers. (How this can help you will be mentioned again, in passing.) But, if you're coming to cryptic crosswords for the first time, don't worry. Of course, it does help to have a smidgen of intelligence but you don't have to be an Einstein to think sideways!

---

[1] For the record, the reasoning behind our first poser is as follows. 'Popular' (you will see from our glossary) is a crossword convention for IN. 'Sounding' is another convention meaning 'something that sounds like' — while the 'ghost' in question is SPECTRE. Putting together IN and what sounds like SPECTRE gives INSPECTOR. Then the 'code' in question is MORSE (also in the glossary) which leads to the answer a 'policeman on TV' INSPECTOR MORSE.

So, our assumption in putting this book together is that you are a complete beginner, that you have seen these mysterious things called cryptic crosswords and would like to have some idea how to put letters into the gaping holes. To this purpose, we present the easiest forms first, then progress to the more difficult. Finally, at the end of the book we provide a selection of clues with answers for practice. When you've finished those, then it is up to you. At the end of the day there is no substitute for opening your regular paper at the crossword page and having a go yourself, then next day studying the answers that you couldn't get and trying to understand how they were arrived at.

HEY PRESTO — WELCOME TO THE MAGIC SHOW!

We enjoy the performance of clever stage magicians and illusionists because we like being deceived — or at least we like being deceived while in the safety of a theatre or our own armchair. The crossword compiler and magician have much in common: they are both out to pass our time in an entertaining way and to do so by trying to deceive us.

Illusion and sleight of hand are just as much the tools of the compiler as the magician. While the magician uses wires and physical props, the compiler exploits the nature of the English language. (We'll consider its quirks and how the compiler puts them to advantage later.) In the well-written clue, the compiler creates a scenario that pushes you, amazingly with a mere handful of words, into looking in the wrong direction.

The upshot is you must always remember that you are being presented with a pretence. The compiler is trying to put you under his spell, trying to capture your imagination and lead it his way. So approach every clue with a down-to-earth scepticism. Tell yourself that what you are looking at is not what it seems.

For instance, take:

Mexican food found in catacomb (4) [2]

The compiler is playing two tricks here. Firstly, the phrase 'found in catacomb' suggests the answer is maybe something to do with archaeology. Well, it isn't. Secondly, he has actually presented us with the answer in full view but he has obscured it by wrapping a lot of letters round it. In fact, the answer is a run of letters within the word 'catacomb' — TACO — the celebrated Mexican dish.

Now consider:

Came out on top (4)

The device being used here is the anagram, simply mixing up letters of one word to form another. We know this because of the inclusion of the word 'out', a standard anagram indicator which we will discuss in detail later. So, rearranging the letters in 'Came' we get the answer — ACME — another word for 'top'.

---

[2] Clues which are to be explained in the text (like this one) will be positioned centrally in the page in heavy type. With these you might find you get more from them if you use a piece of card or your bookmark to mask the explanation which is coming up and give the clue a little thought before proceeding.

One final example for the time being:

Power strike (5)

Here we are getting the suggestion of a blackout or maybe trade union action. But that is only the scenario that the compiler is setting up and trying to divert us with, because the answer is CLOUT, which simultaneously means 'strike' in formal English and 'power' in more colloquial speech.

Although the three examples above are rather short and fairly easy as cryptics go, we can get quite a bit of mileage out of them for demonstration purposes. Firstly, they each contain a **definition**, that is, a word or phrase which has the same meaning as the answer, telling us what we should be looking for. In the first, the definition was 'Mexican food'. In the next, it was 'top'. While in the last there were actually two definitions: 'power' and 'strike'.

So now we can extract our first principle. Every clue will contain a **definition**. The snag is it will be disguised — but that is what the game is about. So one of your first tasks in looking at a clue is to identify which bit is the definition. Now, a useful thing to bear in mind here is that in about 80% of cases the definition is either at the beginning or end of the clue. This is particularly useful with a long clue that you might be having a problem with because it means you can temporarily ignore the middle bit. This proportion splits fairly equally with about 40% of clues featuring the definition at the beginning of the clue (like 'Mexican food') and 40% of cases featuring it at the end (as in the case of 'top'). There you go — we've only just started and you've already got a guide to tackling 80% of clues!

Another thing that these examples demonstrate is the notion of the **scenario**, that is a theme running through the clue that provokes a certain image. Now, the scenario can be helpful but is more likely to have been devised to mislead. You might remember we mentioned this earlier when warning of the false direction in which you may be nudged. In the first example above, some archaeological connection was being suggested by the word 'catacomb'. The second was more subtle, suggesting that it was something to do with passing exams or doing well in some sporting contest. The last had the implication of industrial action. In each case this was the scenario — and in each case it was a deliberate diversion — and therefore something we should ignore.

Finally, the first two clues contained an **indicator** of the trick that the compiler was up to. It is a convention of the game that compilers give us some kind of hint of what device they are employing and most of the time they follow the rules. In the first example, the word 'in' indicated that the answer was a run or consecutive series of letters within the clue. In the second, 'out' was the hint that the answer was in the form of an anagram.

So to summarise, from these simple examples we have learned three things:

1. Each clue will contain a **definition**, which most commonly will be at the beginning or the end. (The third example contained two definitions but that particular one is a special kind of clue that we will consider in more depth later.)

2. Well-written clues will present a **scenario**, some kind of 'scene' or general idea that makes sense both grammatically and on its own terms. This can be legitimate but it is more likely to be a smokescreen, the aim of which is to throw you off the scent. (Just as when the magician waves his right hand and says 'Look, nothing in my hand', if we want to know what's going on, we should be looking at his left!)

3. Most clues will contain some kind of **indicator** of the deception that is being employed. An indicator is a coded device letting you know what form the answer will take — an anagram or run and so on.

In the rest of the book, through the use of examples and lots of practice clues, we are going to be looking at the different types of clue, the tricks used to build up diverting scenarios, and the various devices employed to fool us, along with the indicators used by the compiler to drop hints.

WHAT YOU WILL GET OUT OF CROSSWORDS

There are several kinds of enjoyment and benefit derivable from crosswords. The obvious one is the satisfaction from cracking a single clue which for some time has seemed impenetrable. Then of course there is the pleasure derived when you complete a whole grid.

Also, there is the enjoyment of learning new words enhanced by the process of self-discovery, especially when you know you have built up the answer correctly but the resulting word is unfamiliar. For instance, the answer to this next one was new to the writer:

Smart chap holds one duty-list up, as chances appear (9)

From the glossary we can see that ALEC could be the 'smart chap' and ROTA the 'duty-list'. The presence of the word 'up' means that ROTA has to be reversed along with I (i.e. 'one') and the result ATORI inserted into ALEC. (Don't worry if you find this clue difficult. This is the kind of clue we will build up to later.) This gives ALE(ATORI)C = ALEATORIC which a dictionary tells us means 'depending on chance'. If we have not heard of this word, there can be a sense of achievement in getting to the obscure answer off one's own bat.

Along with new words that you will come across, there will be the pleasure of learning new meanings to known words. And of expanding your knowledge of history, geography and so on in a pleasurable way.

Regularly attempting a crossword can give a useful kick-start to one's brain — like doing a few press-ups first thing in the morning. Interestingly on this matter, doctors are now saying that a daily dose of crosswording is a particularly healthy exercise for the brain especially as one gets older — just as regular physical exercise is beneficial to the body.

But we have to say that some pleasure, like the appreciation of a good wine or rare malt whisky, comes only with experience. The corollary in crosswording is the appreciation of a good clue. A clue should be challenging yet solvable. By 'solvable' we mean once you have put in the right answer there is no doubt that it is right — even if you don't know the word (as one might not have been familiar with the word 'aleatoric' earlier). And by 'challenging' we don't mean just difficult. There are some compilers who are difficult just for the sake of it and, one has to admit, completing their grids can be more of a chore than enjoyment. No, the difficulty should be in the form of cleverness, specifically the cleverness in legitimately diverting the punter's attention from the right track.

Next, a clue should read well. This means two things. Firstly, it should have some regard to grammar or at least have a flow. Sad to say, sometimes clues are clumsy. (It has been said that the mark of a badly written clue is that it just looks like a crossword clue — and nothing else.) A second criterion is that the clue embodies a theme throughout its length, a scenario which may or may not have anything to do with the answer. Being able to appreciate this aspect of your opponent's skill comes as icing on the cake.

The following clue measures up to these standards:

One of the Stones, rocking, features a new record to start (5)

This is what you will learn later we call a compound clue, a clue built up with Lego bricks. The Lego bricks in this case are firstly LOG (i.e. record) which we have to place at the beginning as indicated by the phrase 'to start'. This we build up as LOG + A + N (i.e. new) to give the answer LOGAN — which your dictionary will tell you, if like me you didn't know this word either, is 'a poised heavy stone that rocks at a touch'.

The form of the clue is quite standard but its cleverness lies in the use of 'Stones', 'rocking' and 'a new record'. At first bluff it is impossible to read it without thinking of pop music and a certain long-lived rock band — yet the answer has nothing to do with the pop world at all. If Oscars were given for good clues, this one should be in the running.

SOME TECHNICAL JARGON

You don't need to know crossword jargon to solve cryptics but, as with anything else, some technical words are helpful when discussing the basics, so here we go. The puzzle itself is usually called a **grid**. Most commonly the grid consists of open squares (called **lights**) and blacked-in squares, the latter marking the beginnings and ends of words. A little less often, the whole of the grid consists of lights while the beginnings and ends of words are signified by thick lines instead of black squares.

The answers for the first set of clues (ACROSS) will read like ordinary print from left to right. The second lot of answers (clues listed under DOWN) will read vertically downward. The letters shared by Across and Down solutions (where they cross) are called **checked letters**; those letters belonging uniquely to one answer are called **unchecked** letters. Whether a clue is 'Across' or 'Down' can be important as it can have implications for how we should interpret the clue. For instance, in an 'Across' clue the word 'up' can only have its regular dictionary meaning, whereas in a 'Down' clue it can take on a separate significance as an instruction for us to reverse a component.

For completeness, we recap the main technical terms we have met:

definition — a word or phrase which is contained in the clue and will have the same meaning as the answer

scenario — the overall 'scene' painted by the clue, which can be helpful or deliberately misleading

indicator — a coded device (word or phrase) used in the instructions telling us how to construct the solution.

CLUE TYPES

The word **cryptic** itself comes to us through both Greek and Latin with the meaning of 'hidden', and is the same root that gives us crypt for a hidden chamber. And a cryptic crossword, the Oxford Dictionary tells us, is one which indicates the answers 'in a way that is not straightforward'. (Not straightforward — as you might already have gathered — can be an understatement!)

This element of trickery puts the cryptic puzzle in direct opposition to the **definitional** type (variously known as 'Simple', 'Concise', 'Quickie' or 'Coffee-Break'), which is straightforward and solely requires knowledge to solve. Adherents of one type of puzzle should not be scornful of the other. (I'm afraid they can be.) Both types of teaser have their purpose. The definitional puzzle, as its alternative labels suggest, provides a relatively short diversion. In the general press the knowledge required to complete a definitional is restricted to knowledge of everyday language. In a specialist magazine the definitional can be based on knowledge of the area covered by the publication (pop music, television, real ale or whatever). On the other hand, the cryptic provides an amusement that is more in the nature of a game; and, with the exception of an enviable few, takes the average punter more time to solve!

A SHORT DIVERSION ON THE US CROSSWORD

In the main, the last comment in the above paragraph applies to the British-style cryptic as found in the UK and some other countries such as Australia and India. In the United States, where the crossword was invented and began its long-term popularity, puzzles are still largely definitional with clues of only a few words each. Contrary to the aforementioned remark, this does not mean they take less time to solve because the American version makes up for its straightforwardness by sheer size. Compared to the norm of around twenty-eight clues in a British broadsheet, the crosswords in US leading newspapers such as *The New York Times* and *Washington Post* have upwards of a hundred clues!

They have different conventions too. Their grids contain a smaller proportion of black squares so that most of the letters are checked, the result of which is that by answering half the questions you virtually finish the grid. Also they are quite happy to include solutions that are not words, such as SSS as the answer to 'Adder alarm' which would not be acceptable to compilers or solvers in most UK puzzles. Another difference that the British will find strange is that the number of letters in the answer is not appended to the clue. This might not seem too drastic, but it can present a problem when you don't know that the answer is made up of several words.

Returning to the British form, cryptics can be grouped into five categories:

1. **The standard cryptic** — which is its most common form of clue and consists of two parts: a definition and a set of instructions for finding the answer. This can be **simple**, usually short, embodying one component and instruction. Or it can be what we call a **compound**, where the instructions involve several components with an accompanying assortment of indicators.

2. **The single definition** — this is relatively rare and consists of a single definition, typically only two words, which has the appearance of a simple 'quickie' clue but actually embodies a cryptic element.

3. **The double definition** — in which two definitions are given side by side, with or without instruction, the two definitions being synonymous with each other.

4. **The double duty clue** — here the whole clue does double duty, simultaneously being the definition *and* the set of instructions for finding the answer. (This can also be called the '**& lit**' clue, so named because you have to read the clue twice: first to identify the instructions, then you have to read the whole thing again, this time *literally*, in order to get the definition.)

5. **The whimsical clue** — this contains only a definition and nothing else, the definition being based on some kind of pun. (Also called the '**cryptic definition**' type; but the label 'whimsical' has the virtue of embodying the notion of a caprice or playfulness — as in music a caprice is a playful work of art — and playfulness is what puns are all about!)

Whichever terms you choose to use, these notions are important because one of the first jobs when facing a clue is identifying to what category it belongs. It is essential for you to know what you are looking at from the outset and in a later chapters we shall be looking at each in turn.

PLAYING BY THE RULES

Although there is no governing body running the crossword world, several conventions have evolved over the years and most compilers try to abide by them.

1. Every clue must contain a **definition** — something, which describes or gives the meaning of the solution, so you know what you are looking for.

2. Every clue must contain **only those words that are necessary** for finding or confirming the answer. There must be nothing superfluous just to make the answer look pretty or read easily; this means of course that nothing extra must be introduced merely to throw the solver. All deception should be embodied in clever wording.

3. Every clue must contain enough information for the answer to be **uniquely right** — that is, once you have found the answer that complies with the information that you have been given, there must be no question that it is right.

4. Any of the first three rules can be broken[3].

EQUIPMENT FOR THE JOB

The beginner, and veteran if it comes to that, needs to have a handful of reference books handy. Now, there is a feeling amongst many solvers that the use of books, etc. is in some way cheating. There is no need to be burdened by such qualms. Of course, there will be expert solvers who will pride themselves on finishing a 'posh paper' cryptic with no use of aids, but these lucky people must be a minority, an enviable elite. Bearing in mind that the compiler has many books and aids at his disposal when setting the puzzle, why should the common-or-garden solver (like the writer and the readers of this book) be at a disadvantage?[4]

So you need:

1. a standard **dictionary**, the bigger and the more up to date the better. Obviously you can only use a dictionary if you already know what you are looking for, so the main function of your dictionary will be for confirming spelling. However, it can also be used for checking the existence of a word that you've never heard of. 'Aleatoric' comes to mind again.

Another valuable use for dictionaries is to search for some combination or phrase, provided you know the first word. For example, say you are faced with

Office announcement about leave (5,10)

and the letters you already have suggest that the first word might be 'state' but you are at a loss with regard to how to complete it. Looking under 'state' in your dictionary for a two-word phrase whose last term is ten letters you will find STATE DEPARTMENT — and you're there. (At the moment we are not concerned with how the answer is built up but if you want to know the reasoning see below.[5])

2. a **thesaurus**, which will provide synonyms. The original thesaurus was compiled by Roget and is kept up to date by Penguin, but there are several versions on the market.

The above two are all you need to get going but eventually you will find the following useful:

---

[3] A slight exaggeration. Only Rules 2 and 3 get blatantly broken. Rule 1 gets bent occasionally.

[4] Innovatory gadgetry has not stopped with the pocket electronic Crossword machine. There are programs (for example on the Internet) for helping with anagrams and identifying words with missing letters. Moreover, compilers now have access to programs that actually fill in their grid for them.

[5] Construction of STATE DEPARTMENT. 'Office' is the clue's definition, STATEMENT is the 'announcement', while 'leave' is DEPART. 'about' is given in our glossary as a nesting indicator instructing us that the former should encircle the latter thus: STATE(DEPART)MENT to give STATE DEPARTMENT, the government office of foreign affairs).

3. a **UK Gazetteer** (for example, an AA book) as almost any town and village in the UK is fair game. Also be warned: some knowledge of London landmarks and suburbs, not to mention Underground stations and lines, is assumed. So some kind of map of the capital will not come amiss.

4. **Brewer's Dictionary of Phrase and Fable**. This is invaluable as a reference work on Classical Mythology and a whole range of literary and linguistic material.

5. a **book of quotations**. Not essential but you will get the occasional quotation thrown at you. But don't be too worried because the quotes will be well-known ones.

6. anything with **elementary** French, German, Spanish, etc. (say, a tourist phrase book) as compilers are prone to include basic words from the major languages when they have a mind to. However, the most common borrowings from foreign tongues are restricted to definite and indefinite articles and a handful of simple words.

7. a **book of lists**, usually with 'Crossword' in the title. Such a book not only gives all kinds of lists (flowers, capitals, mountains, etc.) but does so very helpfully in order of word-length. See, for example, *Crossword Lists*, published by Bloomsbury Publishing. Also, some of these books (and some dictionaries) list **abbreviations**, which figure constantly in cryptics. In this category, we could mention the *Pocket Crossword Dictionary* (Bloomsbury Publishing) which specialises in just those short words that are amenable to being used as components in compound clues.

8. finally, the kind of books that you might find on the family bookshelf — **an atlas, the Bible, history books, general knowledge books, the works of Shakespeare** and so on — will not come amiss. The characters created by Messrs Shakespeare and Dickens are regular cast members on the crossword stage. See *Exit, pursued by a bear*, an A-Z guide to Shakespeare's plays and characters published by Bloombury Publishing.

Incidentally, don't be put off by the length of the above list. One or two books you probably have already and you can pick up the others piecemeal.

A daily dose of cryptic puzzle solving not only keeps the mind active — and you'll be surprised how many people you meet who share your pastime once you get into the swing of it — it is also an ongoing educational experience. That is why it is no sin to use the back-up of reference books and other aids.

Interestingly, it is one of the constant pleasures of crossword solving that, after hitting a brick wall with a particular grid and putting the thing aside for a while, a critical answer can come easily when one returns to it. As in other areas of activity, the value to the mind of a break is a mysterious but real phenomenon. Still a mystery to psychologists as to its exact workings, the phenomenon seems to come about either because a break allows the brain to come at a problem from a different angle, or during the break the subconscious still works on the problem in some mysterious way.

Finally, there is a clear pecking order in terms of difficulty with regard to the different national newspapers. Generally, the more popular the paper, the easier is the paper's cryptic. So, the beginner may choose to start with a tabloid but there is enough in this book for the novice to start with one of the broadsheets — the 'Ivy League' of cryptics.

SUMMARY

1. Remember that in the majority of cases the synonym for the answer is the **first** or **last** part of the clue.

2. Ignore the obvious. Remember that the setter is trying to trap you with the obvious, so look for a **less** obvious meaning.

3. Consider each word **separately**, especially when the words have been made to look as if they go together.

4. Be on the lookout for the code words and phrases that serve as indicators.

5. When you reach an impasse with a particular grid, don't lose your cool and give up. Just put it aside for a while, do something else and return to it at another convenient time. Remember, these things are supposed to be fun.[6]

The next chapter may be skipped on a first reading. It does contain some useful crosswording points but, if you are in a hurry, you may prefer to bypass it for the moment and return to absorb its contents at your leisure.

---

[6] All these tips can be seen as practical examples of the lateral thinking approach, namely encouraging your brain to come at a problem from a different angle.

Chapter 2

ENGLISH — WHAT MAKES THE LANGUAGE SO HANDY FOR CROSSWORDING

As an introduction to exploring this area, consider for a few moments the following quartet of clues and try to discover what they have in common:

1. **Support a partner in a way that is permitted (7)**

2. **A friend getting married in UNESCO? (7)**

3. **China set for one at sea? (7)**

4. **Mate comes back with best microcomputer (6)**

As you are a beginner, you will be forgiven if you cannot yet see the connection. Let us look at each in turn and you may spot a link before we reach the end of the exercise. Do not be overly concerned if you find the analysis of the clues too much at this early stage as we are mainly looking at them to make a point. So here we go — the first clue is solved as follows. 'Support' is common crossword code for LEG while 'partner' cues ALLY. Simply pushing them together we get LEG+ALLY = LEGALLY which is defined as 'in a way that is permitted'.

No. 2: Here, the letter A is to be used as it stands and you will see from the glossary that 'married' is standard code for M. In between those two letters we simply insert CRONY (a word standing for 'friend') and we get A + CRONY + M = ACRONYM. An acronym is a word formed from the initial letters of other words and the clue gives us a well-known example, UNESCO, as a guide to what we are looking for.

No. 3: 'China' is famously Cockney rhyming slang for MATE. A 'set' is a group or, as here, LOT. Pushing them together we get MATE + LOT = MATELOT, which is another word for sailor or 'one at sea', our target definition and so our answer.

No. 4: This one presents us with 'Mate', suggesting the word PAL which, when made to come 'back' or be reversed as the clue instructs, becomes LAP. The 'best' of something can be described as the TOP and, running the two words together, we get LAP + TOP = LAPTOP, a 'microcomputer'.

Within four clues we have partner, ally, friend, crony, china, mate and pal. You've guessed it — the common link between the words, and therefore the link between the four clues, is that they all revolve around the notion of 'friend'.

WHAT A LOT OF FRIENDS WE HAVE!

As we now have seven words that are related in meaning, let us consider for a moment what other words we can use to describe a friend or a person who is close to us in the sense of someone being 'on our side'. A few more minutes pondering provides the list below.

abettor (AN)	cobber (Aus; NZ)	friend (G)
accessory (L)	cock (ON)	guardian (O Fr)
accomplice (O Fr)	collaborator (L)	helper (G)
acquaintance (O Fr)	colleague (L)	intimate (L)
adherent (L)	companion (L) [3]	mate (G)
advocate (L)	complice (O Fr)	mucker (Scand)
aide(e)	comrade (L)	oppo (L) [5]
ally (O Fr)	confederate (L)	pal (R, Tk)
amigo (Sp/US)	confidante (L)	pardner (US)
ancillary (L)	confrere (O Fr)	partner (L)
assistant (O Fr)	conspirator (L)	patron (L)
associate (L)	co-worker (L + G)	protector (L)
auxiliary (L)	crony (Gk) [4]	sidekick (O Fris, G)
backer (G)	defender (O Fr)	subordinate (L)
brother (G)	digger (Aus; NZ)	supporter (L)
buddy (US)	fellow-member (ON)	sympathizer (Gk)
china [1]	fellow-worker (ON)	
chum (L + Gk) [2]	follower (G)	

The first thing we notice about the list is the large number of close synonyms for friend or someone who is on our side — there are over fifty — each word with its own subtle difference in meaning from the others. Some are quite formal, some are more associated with criminal friendliness (e.g. 'accessory'), some are colloquial and one case in particular ('cock') is virtually restricted to greetings between males. Interestingly, although the notion of 'friend' was taken at random for this exercise, you will find that over a dozen of the words in the table make regular appearances in crosswords — we have seen seven already — and once you have embarked upon your own puzzle-solving you can be expected to make a link to any of the remainder too! (For that reason, when you've finished our little book, you may wish to return to the list from time to time for your own purposes. In the meantime — if you feel up to it yet — you can have a go at some examples given on page 96, all using words from the above table.)

Secondly, from the key given at the end of the chapter we will observe the wide range of languages from which they are drawn. The synonyms for just the one word 'friend' come from **fourteen** distinct tongues. Even a traditional Romany word like 'pal' has been seconded for service in everyday English. So, the language is rich in synonyms because of the wide number of tongues from which it has drawn.

THE ORIGINS OF ENGLISH

Of all the main languages, English is probably unique in the wide contact it has had with other languages. In the first instance, this is because of the varied invasions and waves of immigrants that have marked the history of the British Isles, each leaving an indelible stamp on the language. So the English we speak today is a glorious mish-mash showing clear signs of the original Celt settlers, the Romans, the varied Germanic incomers, the Vikings, then the Norman-French. Subsequently Britain has been home to many groups of outsiders fleeing persecution — Jews, French Huguenots for example — each contributing new words to English.

Also of significance is Britain's more recent history of colonial expansion. This brought English into contact with languages further afield, particularly the two hundred years political association with India through which words like bungalow, pukka and many more were taken on board. (Later on we will come across an extremely good clue the answer to which is verandah, which comes straight to us from Hindustani.)

Along the way, English absorbed from other languages too. Ponder for a moment on:

Ski OK, however crashing into small shop (5)

This is a straightforward anagram clue instructing us (through the anagram indicator 'crashing') to rearrange the letters of 'Ski OK' to give us a 'small shop' — KIOSK. We may use this word regularly without realising it has been appropriated from Turkish. (The word coffee was snaffled from the Turks too.)

Moreover, the language has borrowed wholesale from Arabic — from whence come admiral, zero, zenith, nadir, and algebra, not to mention our **whole** numbering system! Think about it. If it wasn't for the Arabs we would still be stuck with Roman numerals and to give you an idea of what problems that would present us with today, see how far you get trying to multiply XXIV by MCIII. However, we still retain Roman numerals for some labelling purposes — a remnant of British history that gives crossword compilers an extra box of ammunition, as demonstrated by the following:

Numbers of Romans about the city (5)

This is a really clever clue because the **entire** answer is made up of Roman numerals — CIVIC, meaning 'about the city'. In any one particular grid it is highly likely that you will be expected to use at least one of the following: I, V, X, L, C, D or M. (So if you've forgotten any of them, now's the time to brush up on their meanings.)

In modern times, the English language baton has been picked up by the United States. Its own history has provided words from the original Americans (formerly Red Indians), words which have been simply absorbed into the everyday speech of English speakers around the world and thereby into crosswords, as witnessed by:

The prisoner met with sensational success at the conference (3-3)

This emerges as POW ('prisoner' as in prisoner-of-war) plus WOW ('sensational success') to give POW-WOW, a 'conference'. Today we may say 'the bosses are having a pow-wow' with little thought to the origins of 'pow-wow' way back in the tepees on the Prairie. Then, through slavery, African words were adapted and absorbed into American English — jazz, juke (hence jukebox), jam (giving us jam session) and many more. At this point we could note that there is some evidence that the ubiquitous OK (okay) came to us unaltered from an African coastal language.[1]

Finally, through commerce and the Internet, it is the American version of English that is now dominant around the world. It is unfortunate that many British people gripe at what appears as a modern invasion of American spelling — without realising that over the last two centuries they have already quite happily accepted American spellings for many words (long ago dropping the British spellings of publick, gaol and cyder in favour of the American public, jail and cider, for example).

The implications of the evolution of English for the crossworder are manifold. We have already demonstrated its richness in synonyms, which makes the compiler's job easier — and your job as the solver more difficult!

Some people carp at the seemingly anarchic spelling of English and there have been countless attempts to standardise it over the centuries. However, there are several reasons why spelling can be so varied. For a start, in the early days of printing there were no dictionaries so each printer used his own version of a word and many of these oddities persist to the present day. But aside from these quirks, differences arose because of the different linguistic sources of words. Such words which sound alike but have different spellings are called homophones and the crossword compiler has a field day with them, witness:

Use your teeth to cut the loop (4)

This is playing with the words BITE (which is the answer) and BIGHT. Now, would-be standardizers of the language argue that it is about time that we spelled them the same because they have the same pronunciation. Yet it is important to retain the difference between them because they have different meanings. BIGHT which is related to 'bow', means a bend in a geographical feature such a river or

---

[1] In its own right OK is a useful letter combination in crosswords to build answers like POKE, HOKUM, JOKER, etc. So be on your guard when compilers use words like 'fine' 'all right' and 'good' in a crossword clue, they can be code for you to insert OK.

coast (hence 'loop' in the clue), while BITE stems from the German *beissen* meaning to cut with the teeth. Take another:

Pour from the side, you say (4)

Now, the answer is TEEM ('pour') because it sounds like a 'side' i.e. TEAM. The reason why these two words are spelled differently is because TEEM came to English via the Vikings while TEAM (suggested by 'side') has a different and more direct Germanic root.

THE EVOLUTION OF LANGUAGE

Few words have fixed meanings and, like all languages, the English that we use changes following observable principles. One of these is the process of **specialization**. As an example, there was a time when 'undertaker' like the French *entrepreneur* simply meant a contractor, somebody who undertakes to do a particular piece of work of any kind. However, in English for some unknown reason it has become confined exclusively to mean an undertaker of funerals. But I have come across at least one clue that expected the solver to be aware of the older general meaning. (Incidentally, our American cousins spotted this dilemma years ago and solved it by inventing 'mortician'.)

Similarly:

Edible part of fruit with tea, for example, provides intense source of enjoyment (4,3,5)

The answer required for this one is MEAT AND DRINK, i.e. a figurative term for 'intense source of enjoyment'. What has happened here is that 'meat' formerly meant **any** kind of food but has become specialized in modern times to mean only edible flesh. However, in its archaic sense it is still retained in odd pockets such as sweetmeat and, of course, 'meat and drink'. So beware — compilers are very aware of these linguistic fossils and will make use of them to trip you up.

The above example demonstrated a definite shift in meaning over time but a word's use can be extended to cover other meanings while the original is kept in the language. This process is known as **extension** of meaning and will lead to one word having several separate meanings — and predictably provides the compiler with much of his ammunition. For example:

Show friendliness to give support (4)

The answer to this is BEAM ('support') which originally came to us from *Baum*, German for tree or wood. Sometime ago our ancestors extended the word to mean 'stretch' — through the notion of stretching something along a bough or beam. Indeed, in the clothing industry to 'beam' still means to stretch cloth over a beam. Then picturesque speech drew the analogy to stretching one's mouth across one's face to produce a smile, 'to beam' — a way to 'show friendliness' as it is worded in the clue. And, by the linguistic process of extension, it's only a hop, skip and a jump to 'Beam me up, Scottie'. (To understand further the phenomenon of extension in language, think for a moment how Captain Kirk's 'beam' relates to the meanings we have already considered.)

On the other hand, we can get a word having several meanings through simple accidents in spelling which have then become enshrined in our language. This is a quirk compilers will use as in the following:

Riding establishment boss (4)

The answer to this is STUD which relates to 'riding' through its origin in German *Stute* (mare) and from which we get our word 'steed', hence the 'riding establishment' of the clue. But, from the same source, we also borrowed *Stutzen*, which means prop or support and which, way back in the mists of time, somebody changed to STUD, meaning a prop or 'boss'. So now we have one word with two different meanings.

And there is another crucial development that is a boon to the setters of crosswords. Over the last 1500 years English has dropped many of its inflexions. Its parent languages — Anglo-Saxon, Old German, Latin, etc. — were all **inflected**, that is to say special endings were attached to words identifying what type of word it was and its role in the sentence. German has kept its endings up to this day so just by looking at a word you generally know if it is a noun or verb and so on. For good or bad, English has let most of this go, so that in many instances you don't know what a word means or what role it has until you see it in context, that is sitting in a sentence. If you are still at a loss about this, just ask yourself how many times have you heard someone questioning the meaning of an English word and the other person responding, not with an answer, but with another question: 'What's the context?'

But what is a loss to English speakers is a positive gain to crossword compilers. They are forever kidding us that a word is a verb, say, and we are utterly stumped until we realise it's being used as a noun. It could never happen in an inflected language like German. Look at this one:

Many, to the stranger, seem decrepit (6)

What parts of speech have we been presented with? 'Stranger' is a noun, 'seem' is a verb and 'decrepit' is an adjective. It's obvious, isn't? But is it? Look again. One of them has been given false clothing. Cunningly, the compiler has dressed 'stranger' up as a noun but it's actually an **adjective** that we should be thinking of. That adjective is ODDER to which we have to add a large number (i.e. 'Many'). The large number is D (500, Roman numerals again) leading us to D + ODDER = DODDER, which is what we do when we 'seem decrepit' as the clue so quaintly puts it.

On the other hand, a noun can be dressed up as a verb, as in this one:

Care to add Russian cash to Thai capital? (7)

'Care', clearly a **verb** in the context of the clue, suggests 'nurse' or 'look after'. Hitting a dead end with that interpretation we might consider 'Care to ... ?' which suggests 'Would you like to ... ?' Wrong again. We have to interpret it in isolation as a **noun**. Only in that way can we get at the answer TROUBLE — built by adding T (Thai capital) to ROUBLE (Russian cash).

Here's one for you to try:

Stop in US in charge of regular returns (8)　　　　　　　　　　[271]

Some guidance: 'stop' could be a verb but in fact it's part of a noun phrase, So you need to think of a noun, a special word that means a 'stop in US'. (Another hint: what in the UK is called a 'full stop'). To that you need to add a standard two-letter abbreviation for 'in charge' to get the answer. (Incidentally, the number in square brackets on the right of the clue shows you where you can check the solution in the answer section. Throughout the book, all practice clues have such a key.)

Finally, English today is probably more dynamic than it has ever been. Having become the world language (in the sense of having most speakers whether as first or second language), it is subject to more influences than it has ever known. Apart from subtle changes in its grammar and structure brought to it by non-native speakers and by the requirements of worldwide electronic communication, the number of new words being added daily is literally countless.

One saving grace here for the poor solver is that compilers tend to be a little, let us say, mature, so the 'meat and drink' of the crossword doesn't change quite as much as language in the outside world. (You will have noticed that 'meat and drink' has cropped up again, this time meaning basics.) New words are a little slower coming into the grids while old ones remain in vogue a little longer than they probably should. (In fact, sometimes one feels that, in the world of crosswords, time is actually standing still. For instance, while trawling recent grids in search of examples to go into this book there have been several instances where I have come across 'Ted' for unruly youth and 'beehive' for a hair style — both words probably meaningless to anyone who didn't live through the 1950s!)

One last observation: it has occurred to me while producing the present work that doing cryptic crosswords would be an admirable way for learners of English — say those at an intermediate or advanced level — to expand their understanding of the language. They would certainly be brought into contact with many of its subtleties and nuances.

So, to native speakers and foreigners alike, let us glory in the language, the language of Shakespeare and the Internet — not least through crosswording!

AN	Anglo-Norman	O Fr	Old French
Aus	Australian	O Fris	Old Frisian
G	Germanic (inc. Saxon, Dutch etc.)	R	Romany
Gk	Greek	Sp	Spanish
L	Latin	Tk	Turkish
NZ	New Zealand	Scand	Scandinavian
ON	Old Norse	US	United States

[1] Cockney rhyming slang, in full *china plate*. (Interestingly, the origin of the name of the country China itself is unknown. One thing that is known is that it is *not* native Chinese!)

[2] short for *chamber-fellow* originally Oxford University slang

[3] *com* (Latin for with) + *panis* (Latin for bread) so a companion is someone with whom you 'break bread'

[4] originally Cambridge University slang and meaning a fellow student of one's own year, i.e. someone who is *chronologically* the same

[5] abbreviation of *opposite number*, originally military slang

Chapter 3

THE BASIC TRICKS

In this section we get down to the nitty-gritty and look at the devices that compilers use. As we are still in the early stages of our understanding of cryptics, each trick will be looked at in isolation and demonstration clues have been chosen accordingly.

THE RUN

This is the only kind of clue that comes to you served on a plate. Some call it the 'hidden' clue but here we prefer 'run' because that is exactly what it is: a run or consecutive series of letters. In its simple form it's clear to see within the words of the clue so it certainly isn't hidden — remember TACO in 'catacomb'? (Others call it the 'buried word' which is also appropriate.)

For example, if asked to find a three-letter word for a 'bone' in TRIBUTE, we should see RIB pretty quickly. Or, if asked to identify 'entrances' in LEGATESHIP, we shouldn't have much difficulty in picking out GATES. It can be as easy as that.

To let you know it's a run, the compiler will use a run indicator. These are words or phrases embodying the notion of a **run**, so they will use words like 'series' or 'sequence'; or suggesting that the answer is **inside** with terms like 'among', 'seen in' or just 'in'; or indicating that the answer is **part of** what precedes or follows, so words like 'some' or 'part of' will be the sign. See if you can spot the run in:

Depressed among clowns? (3)

If you can pick out LOW you shouldn't have any trouble with identifying runs. Here's some for you to try. (Remember, all practice clues have a number in square brackets on the right hand side, showing you where you can find the correct solution in the answer section.)

Expert in tracery (3)   [042]

A	C	E

Colour of credibility (3)   [261]

R	E	D

Relax with leasehold (4)   [173]

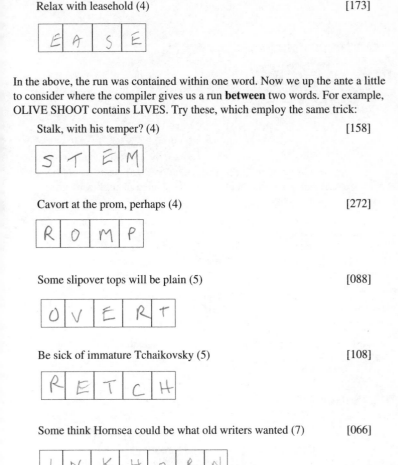

| E | A | S | E |

In the above, the run was contained within one word. Now we up the ante a little to consider where the compiler gives us a run **between** two words. For example, OLIVE SHOOT contains LIVES. Try these, which employ the same trick:

Stalk, with his temper? (4)   [158]

| S | T | E | M |

Cavort at the prom, perhaps (4)   [272]

| R | O | M | P |

Some slipover tops will be plain (5)   [088]

| O | V | E | R | T |

Be sick of immature Tchaikovsky (5)   [108]

| R | E | T | C | H |

Some think Hornsea could be what old writers wanted (7)   [066]

| I | N | K | H | O | R | N |

Because, on the face of it, runs are fairly easy, compilers will employ a couple of subterfuges. The first one is to try to throw you off the scent that it is a run in the first place usually by a contrived scenario. The second trick is to build in some complications but we will look at these later on. So, the upside is they're relatively undemanding; the downside, for the same reason, is you're unlikely to get more than one in a particular grid, at least outside of the 'quickie' puzzles. Nevertheless, *that one* can be the first clue you can answer when starting a new grid and so it can provide you with some letters to get you going on others.

The main problem therefore with the run type of clue is simply recognising that it is one. For example, the following could have you stumped until you recognise them for what they are, simple runs:

Sell lavender after repeated pruning (4)   [201]

Buried in haste, although secrecy will be evident (7)   [053]

In most cases, but not all, a run will be signposted by a special indicator. The run indicators in the above clues in order were: **in, of, with, at, some, could be, after repeated pruning, buried in**. These and other common indicators are given below:

RUN INDICATORS

among	grabs	pruning	some
buried in	grabbed by	sample of	some extent, to
area of	in	section of	with
at	keeps	seen in	
circumscribed	kept by	sequence	
could be	part of	series	

For more practice examples of run type clues, see page 86.

THE ANAGRAM

The most popular device used by all cryptic compilers must be the anagram. Having fun playing around with letters goes back to Ancient Greeks, in fact the word itself is theirs — ANA (anew) + GRAMMA (letters). With it, one transposes the letters of one word to construct another word, as in the example we met earlier when CAME had to be reassembled into ACME. There are many others: MADE can become DAME; and then there's DEAL/LEAD, STEAM/MATES, THREE/THERE and so on.

The following is a good starting example:

Unusual pear harvest (4)

It has a scenario relevant to the answer, suggesting something to do with agriculture. 'Harvest' is the definition and 'Unusual' tells us we have to make an anagram of PEAR. Shuffling the letters we get REAP, an answer in keeping with the agricultural theme.

Your cue that this is the particular game being played by the compiler will usually be an anagram indicator. In the above example it was 'unusual'. No complete list of anagram indicators could possibly be given but they will take the form of suggesting that a word is, or has to be, **broken** ('smash', 'smashed', 'hammered'), **re-assembled** ('sort', 'sorted', 'order'), **worked on** ('modelled', 'formed', 'revised', 'somehow', 'sorted'), **not right** ('crazy', 'off', 'muddled', 'unusual', 'wrong') or **affected** ('posing'). More subtle but common forms appear as 'perhaps', 'maybe', 'possibly', 'potentially'. To confuse you further the compiler will use what looks like a run indicator such as 'seen in'. Even worse, in some cases no obvious indicator is given apart from a question or exclamation mark to let you know something is amiss — if you are lucky.

In the following, the compiler is using 'incorrectly' as the anagram indicator:

Decree incorrectly cited? (5)

to give the answer EDICT, fitting the definition 'Decree'.

See how you get on with these anagrams (the key for checked letters is at the end of the chapter):

Possibly sent home (4) [280]

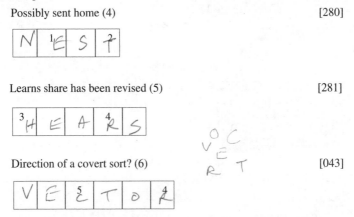

Learns share has been revised (5) [281]

Direction of a covert sort? (6) [043]

Hopefully you could answer them — but did you take note of the anagram indicators used in each case? They were 'possibly', 'revised' and 'sort'. Remember them, because compilers will be throwing those code words at you when you are out in the wide world solving puzzles on your own.

A little more adventurously, the compiler can throw **two** words at you for re-assembly, as in:

Dampen Tim's one, maybe? (7)

The anagram indicator is 'maybe' telling us that we have to re-assemble TIMS ONE to yield a synonym for 'Dampen' — namely MOISTEN. Now here are some two-worders for you to try. (As our anagrams are getting longer, a useful tip when tackling them is simply to begin by writing down the relevant letters in reverse order to give you a new perspective on possible letter combinations — lateral thinking again.)

The rat poses a menace! (6)　　　　　　　　　　　　[067]

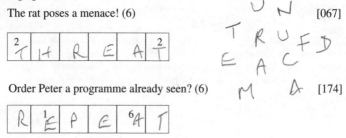

Order Peter a programme already seen? (6)　　　　　[174]

A shade more difficult is when the two words to be re-ordered are **not** adjacent. Hopefully they will be linked by 'and' or 'with' as in the following:

Probable key with ill needing treatment (6)　　　　　[005]

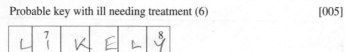

Unfortunately, that is not the end of the story because you can be thrown **three** words to juggle with! Naturally, with more than two, you have more work to do and the required answers are going to be longer. Here are three such trios:

Ely clock I altered produces a thousand revolutions (9)　　[058]

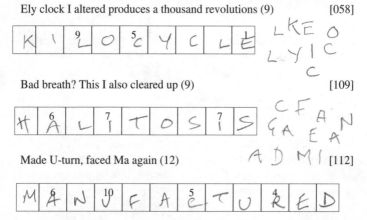

Bad breath? This I also cleared up (9)　　　　　　　[109]

Made U-turn, faced Ma again (12)　　　　　　　　　[112]

Because an anagram presents quite enough of a challenge in itself, in virtually all cases some notification that an anagram is required will be signposted by a special indicator. Anagram indicators in the above clues included 'altered' and 'again'. As we said earlier, the possibilities are extensive but here are a few common ones.

ANAGRAM INDICATORS			
affected	hammered	ordered	smash
altered	ill	out	smashed
broken	jumping	perhaps	somehow
cleared up	jumpy	posing	sort
composed	knocked about	possibly	sorted
crazy	lax	potentially	treated
difficulties in	modelled	re-assembled	treatment, needing
exercising	muddled	re-ordered	unusual
fitfully	nasty	re-worked	working
formed	off	re-used	wrestling

More practice with anagrams can be found on page 87.

HOMOPHONES

Homophones, or sound-alikes, are words that are generally pronounced the same but are spelled differently and have different meanings. Because it has drawn on so many other languages, each with its own spelling forms (see Chapter 2), modern English abounds with examples and we saw a couple earlier in BITE and BIGHT.

So, in these clues we have to think of two separate words. The first one we have to think of will be our stepping-stone to the second which will be the answer. Normally the setter will place a homophone indicator alongside 'the stepping stone' word as in:

Gun law, reportedly (6)

'Reportedly' is the homophone indicator and, placed alongside 'law', means we have to think of a word for 'law', then a similar-sounding word meaning gun. The answer is CANNON — which has the same pronunciation as the technical word for church law, CANON.

There are many indicators of homophones, all to do with sound or speech, 'reportedly' fulfilling the function in the above clue. We can have direct indicators such as 'sound', 'soundly', 'stated', 'proclaimed', 'orally' and so on. And we can have indirect indicators such as 'broadcast', 'on the radio', 'on the air' or 'according to rumour'. (Note how they are all variations on the notion of *sound*.)

One problem with sound-alikes is that if the indicator is placed in the middle of the clue, as occasionally happens, there will be some ambiguity, as in the following:

Put up sound beams (4)

Here, 'sound' is the indicator that we are to look for a pair of homophones, one meaning 'put up' and the other meaning 'beams'. It doesn't take too much thinking to come up with RAISE and RAYS. However, 'sound' is adjacent to both words but our guide that, out of the two, RAYS is the answer is the knowledge that the solution has four letters.

By their nature, homophones tend to be rather short words, as in the above examples, but there are a few longer specimens and they do appear with some regularity as:

Fundamental truth college head proclaimed (9)

The answer is PRINCIPLE, which is a sound-alike for PRINCIPAL. (Don't be ashamed if you have trouble distinguishing between these two in everyday life. Even those of us who have had some time in teaching can still mix the two up.)

Here are a few for you to try.

Exercise in woolly jumpers we're told! (3)   [007]

^{10}U	S	^{1}E

Make a jumper for fool, say? (4)   [104]

K	^{11}N	I	^{2}T

Inclined to be fast, we hear? (5)   [257]

L	^{1}E	A	^{11}N	^{2}T

Let out very little, we hear (6)   [070]

L	E	A	^{12}S	^{1}E	D

Cunning little reported (7)   **[196]**

^{12}S	L	E	I	G	^{3}H	^{2}T

So far we've only looked at single-word homophones but *groups* of words can be pronounced the same. Such a phrase can consist of three words but normally it is two, as in:

Having a specific purpose — to provide more wine, say (2,3)

'To provide more wine, say' could be to ADD HOCK, which is a sound-alike for the answer, AD HOC, referring to something with a specific purpose. Here's a two-word homophone for you to try. 'In conversation' alerts us that it is a homophone clue. You have to think of a two-word phrase meaning 'for a joke' which in turn is a one-word sound-alike for 'absorb':

Absorb in conversation for a joke (6)   [291]

I	$\overset{11}{N}$	G	$\overset{+}{E}$	$\overset{12}{S}$	T

HOMOPHONE INDICATORS

audition in	quoted	sounding
broadcast	reportedly	speech, in
conversation, in	rumour	speak, so to
hear, we	said	told, we're
orally	say	verbally
proclaimed	so-called	voiced
pronounced	sound	

More practice with homophones can be found on page 88.

OMISSION

A significant number of small words can be converted to another word simply by dropping a letter. SMELL becomes SELL, TRAIN becomes RAIN and so on. Consequently, the requirement to omit letters to get an answer, or part of an answer, is as common as the anagram and you will find a handful of examples spread throughout a typical cryptic grid. All we have to do is identify an instruction to omit, cut, drop, abandon and we know we have some cutting to do, as in:

Finally abandoned need for resin (3)

'Need' is LACK, we abandon the final letter as instructed and we have LAC, a synonym for 'resin'. The following each require one letter to be dropped:

Almost the first to be prudish (4)   [186]

	4		13

Splashed around in bog endlessly (4)   [265]

	14		13

A special case of dropping one letter is the instance where we have to omit an initial 'h'. This is indicated in several ways, commonly by an apostrophe. For example:

'Otting up food and having a meal (6)

Hotting up suggests the synonym HEATING. The apostrophe at the start of 'Otting means that we have to drop the initial H to give the answer, EATING.

Another common way that we are told to drop an initial 'h' is by reference to London's East End or more directly to Cockney speech, as in:

For Cockney, Cotswolds may present problems (4)   [197]

	9		12

Or we can be required to leave out two letters:

Yearn to find my way out of pain (4)

Here we have to think of STITCH ('pain'), omit the two letters meaning a 'way' (ST for 'street) and we have ITCH ('yearn').

The following requires us to think of a word meaning 'clear'. Then we have to omit two letters to get a synonym for 'flabby'. (In this we can take note of another regular trick: I'd denotes ID.)

Flabby, I'd make it clear (4)   [008]

9		13	

Or we can be required to drop more letters, *even a complete word*:

Elegant US city with no past (4)

The 'US city' is CHICAGO from which we drop AGO ('past') to reach the answer, CHIC, meaning 'elegant'.

Try your hand at the following, which calls for a girl's nickname to be omitted from a nine-letter word for 'practice' (more helpfully, a practice session) to get a word meaning to 'try again' (i.e. as in a court).

Girl, out of practice, have to try again (6)   [295]

4		3			4

Finally, quite a difficult one. Here, you are required to think of a 10 word adjective that would describe a 'contemptible sort of idiot', then omit the indicated word to give a synonym for 'careless'.

Careless, contemptible sort of idiot losing ring (6)   [297]

	9		2		1

OMISSION INDICATORS

abandoned	lacking	not featuring
almost	left	omitting
barred	less	out
cut	lose	passes away
dismissed	losing	short
dropping out	missing	unavailable
has no	not	

REVERSALS

Many words can simply be reversed to produce another (e.g. REED/DEER, LOOT/TOOL, DEVIL/LIVED) and compilers use this device to get answers or components.

Relevant indicators will embody some notion of going back such as 'back' and 'returning'. Or being turned over such as 'over' and 'around' as in:

Sticks around, looking complacent (4)

where 'Sticks' is GUMS which is then turned 'around' to give us 'looking complacent': SMUG.

One for you:

Prevent vessels being knocked over (4)   [014]

	2		15

In DOWN clues the compiler will take advantage of the answer being in a vertical direction and will signify a reversal with 'up', 'rise' or 'raised'. Example:

Judgment raised spirits (4) (DOWN)

The appropriate pairing here is DOOM and MOOD — but you might notice the ambiguity posed by the indicator being adjacent to both. The result is we cannot know which of the two words to put in until we have a checked letter at either the beginning or end. This breaks Rule 3 and unfortunately you will come across this little problem from time to time. The following is a DOWN clue with no ambiguity:

Notice the rise of the spinners (4) (DOWN)   [167]

	15		2

Most reversals, which provide complete answers, are words of only four letters — but there are some longer:

Secure and bring back the components (5)   [283]

12		4		15

And the reversal business doesn't stop at one word. You can be required to reverse two or more. For example, here's a two-worder:

Upset over a description of champagne by traveller (7)

The 'description of champagne' is BRUT and the 'traveller' is REP which, when turned 'over' as a pair, give us PERTURB, 'upset'.

Now a two-worder for you to try:

Not taking girl back to the railway station (6)   [242]

1		12			11

REVERSAL INDICATORS

about	over	rise
around	raised	turning
back	rejected	turning up
backing	retiring	up
going north	retreated	
knocked over	returning	

More practice clues on reversals can be found on page 91.

SLEEPERS — ABSTRUSE SYNONYMS

We noted in Chapter 2 that, because English has borrowed from many other languages, a great number of its words have an abundance of synonyms. To examine how compilers will use this feature to confuse us, let us look at another word: **OFFER**. A selection of words that could be taken as synonyms for 'offer' are presented in the following diagram.

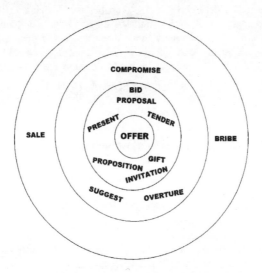

The words in the innermost circle surrounding OFFER are close synonyms and are the first ones that are likely to come to mind. In the next ring are some words that we are likely to think of after a moment's consideration. However, the words in the outer ring are not quite so obvious — but are still justifiable synonyms. This is because they are only synonyms in particular uses. For example, we might not readily think of 'sale' because it is actually the **opposite** of 'gift' which is a close synonym for 'offer'. However, to describe an item as being 'on sale' is very close to saying it is 'on offer'. So in this particular instance, and probably **only** in this instance, the words are in fact reasonable substitutes and a compiler would be justified in linking them.

Similarly, 'bribe' is a very particular kind of 'offer', one with seedy connotations. Without changing his meaning the Godfather could just as well have said 'I gave him a bribe he couldn't refuse' instead of 'I made him an offer he couldn't refuse'. (Needless to say, if Mr Brando had used the more prosaic synonym, the line would not have made it into the pantheon of all-time memorable quotations!)

Words like 'bribe' and 'sale' which are quite legitimate but are out on the periphery we might call *sleeping* synonyms, evoking the sleeper in the espionage game. You may remember he is the agent lying dormant — but waiting to be called into action against the unwary.

The compiler can require us to move in either direction, either inwards to the core or outwards to the periphery. In the following, the word 'lung' could be described as a peripheral word and we have to move *inwards*.

Certified judo practitioner protected lung (5,4)

The answer to this is GREEN BELT. We probably can see that a 'certified judo practitioner' is a 'green belt' but we might be at a loss as to how 'lung' comes into it. However, recourse to a dictionary shows that a 'lung' is an open space in, or close to, a city. So, by a little stretch of the imagination, a 'green belt' can be seen as a 'protected lung'! This relatively obscure connection makes 'lung' a sleeper.

Alternatively, the compiler can require us to move in the opposite direction by giving us the commonplace central word as the clue's definition and requiring us to move *out* to the periphery, to find the sleeper. The following is a good example of this ploy.

The old wrap is swathed round again (3-3)

For a start, it is difficult to identify exactly what part of the clue is the synonym. In fact, it is 'old' — so we are looking for a hyphened adjective with that meaning. (Can you think of one off-hand? I couldn't at first.) So, to get there let us look at the instructions. Firstly, 'again' denotes RE (see the glossary). Then, in this context, 'swathed round' is being used both as an anagram indicator for WRAP **and** as a nesting indicator. Hence we have to nest RE within an anagram of WRAP. This leads us to P(RE)WAR, hence the answer PRE-WAR. When we finally get the answer, we must agree it is quite justifiable as a synonym for 'old', but it certainly isn't the first word we might think of!

On the other hand, a word can be out on the periphery of your mind, not because it is obscure, but because it is a different part of speech. (At least in the last example 'old' and 'pre-war' were both adjectives.) The following contains an old standby, a noun, but the compiler is throwing us off the scent by kidding us it is a verb.

Learner taken to see Dutch artist painting in England (4)

The crucial word is 'see'. Cleverly preceding it by a 'subject' and following it with an 'object' it is difficult for us to avoid taking it as a verb. In fact, 'see' is a popular device in crosswords serving as a cue for the letters ELY, with reference to the religious jurisdiction in Cambridgeshire. Here, combining L ('learner') with ELY we get LELY, the Dutch painter who spent much of his time working in England. So we must be alert to the fact that compilers will take advantage of our natural expectation that a pair of synonyms will be the same part of speech.

We shall finish with an extremely abstruse example. In this one the sleeper is so far out in the boondocks, I will first give you the link to ponder on before we look at the clue. The synonyms or linked words are 'break' and 'beggar'. Can you see the meaning they have in common? Fortunately the clue follows the rules so that we can get the answer without quite knowing where we are going — and be sure that it is right, without knowing immediately why it is right!

Break for something to eat in the tavern (6)

The actual mechanics are not difficult and run as follows. 'Something to eat' is EGG which is then nested within BAR ('tavern') to give us the answer, BEGGAR. But having got this we might have a problem understanding how it relates to the definition 'break'. Some reflection might suggest the phrase 'to beggar your neighbour' which means to do harm to your neighbour and so could be seen as to 'break' your neighbour. Another instance might be the expression 'to beggar belief' which could be re-phrased as to 'break' belief. As you can see, it can be quite a challenge for us to recognise the synonymous connection between 'break' and 'beggar'

So, be on your guard and cast your mind out to the periphery — be on the lookout for sleeping synonyms.

The answer to the following is a sleeper in the sense that it is a technical word (from aero- and astronautics) that has now entered the common vocabulary but you will be unlikely to find a *direct* connection between it and the clue's definition in a thesaurus or dictionary. (Hint: 'thus' is being used as an anagram indicator.)

Having to debar thus, packed in (7)   [009]

6			4		1	

Checked letters

1	2	3	4	5	6	7	8	9	10	11	12	13	14	15
E	T	H	R	C	A	I	Y	L	U	N	S	M	W	P

Chapter 4

TYPES OF CLUE — COMPOUND & NESTING

THE COMPOUND

The compound clue in which the solution is put together like a set of Lego bricks is the most common form of cryptic clue[1]. At its simplest it will take the form of a definition and list of components in the order in which they are to be put together (with no instructions or indicators). So it can be short and straightforward such as:

Attack performing group (5)

Here the clue's definition is 'attack' while 'performing' and 'group' are standard bits of code for ON and SET, which we put together to get the answer, ONSET.

Try this one, which has exactly the same form. All you have to do is think of a word meaning 'party', another meaning 'treat' and put them together to get the answer 'put out'.

Put out party treat (5)   [154]

1		2		3

In compound clues it is common for abbreviations to be used, as in:

Worker's loud complaint (4)

The 'worker' we are concerned with is BEE onto which we tack F ('loud' in music) to get a 'complaint', BEEF.

In the next one, you have to start with a very obvious abbreviation for 'caught' and add a synonym for 'warming up' to get an adjective meaning 'unfair'.

Caught before warming up. It's unfair (8)   [149]

		3		4		5	

---

[1] Along with its nesting variant discussed in the next section.

The compound can have a whole string of components, sometimes as many as five. The following has three. You need a kind of drink (the 'spirit'), to which you add a word from the clue itself and complete the exercise with a 'worker' (another industrious insect, but not a bee this time) to get an adjective meaning 'contemplative'.

Contemplative spirit in worker (8)   [285]

	2		6		7		4

The following clue has four components:

One MP joining city TV supplier is faultless (10)

Its construction goes like this. The first component is I ('one'). The compiler is kind and gives us the next one, MP, in the clue itself. The 'city' is EC (for Empire City, one of New York's nicknames) while the 'TV supplier' is CABLE. Putting them together we get IMPECCABLE or 'faultless'.

Now here's a challenge for you. It is even longer (having five components) but is still straightforward. First, you need to think of a word meaning 'nut' or 'fool', then you repeat it; add two consecutive words straight from the clue itself and finish it off with a word meaning 'spread' to get the target word which means 'taken out'.

A couple of nuts in a spread taken out (12)   [114]

	8		7		8		5		4		1

Finally, the compound method can be used to build up to a whole phrase. The following is a three-word phrase meaning 'feel elated' and is arrived at by adding together a term describing a 'minor part' in a film or play (usually joined by a hyphen) and a verb meaning 'broadcast'.

Feel elated, given minor part on broadcast (4,2,3)   [166]

9			10		5		6	

Further practice clues on the compound type can be found on page 89.

NESTING

The compounds we have examined were straightforward in the sense that their components were delivered to us in their correct order and we had to build up the answer accordingly. But there is no reason they should not be used in any order, for example in reverse.

A common variant of the compound is where one component is placed **inside** another. For this device we borrow the term 'nesting' from computing where the term signifies the embedding of a program into another one. When we are required to nest a word (or component) into another word (or component) we will be given an indicator which denotes embedding in, wrapping round, going inside, going outside, circling and so on. A typical example is where we have to nest a complete word into another complete word such as:

Restoration novel in authentic setting (7)

This calls for nesting NEW (a synonym for 'novel') within REAL (a synonym for 'authentic') to yield RE(NEW)AL = RENEWAL to comply with the definition we have been given, 'restoration'.

In the following, you are required to nest a word meaning 'everyone' within a word meaning 'favour':

Everyone in favour? That's swell! (7)   [010]

	7		11			5

We must remember that even little words that we might overlook can be significant. The following is typical in trying to distract our attention away from the apparently insignificant 'a' by pretending to link it to a noun.

Gather there's a valley round about (5)

However, it is the little word A that we have to nest within GLEN ('valley') — GLE(A)N — to get the answer, GLEAN, a synonym for 'gather'. The following plays the same trick, where you have to think of a word for 'catch' and insert the necessary letter to get an adjective meaning 'in order'.

In order to hold a catch (4)   [192]

5			4

In the following, the nesting indicator ('around') has been camouflaged by presenting it as part of the clause 'rushed around'. So the solution lies in nesting a term for 'dope' within a word meaning 'rushed', to get a synonym for 'caused distress'.

Dope rushed around caused distress (8) [176]

	7			8			1

The next requires you to think of a colloquial term for 'idiot', then nest it within a word meaning 'for example', to get a synonym for 'reason':

Reason, for example, to confine idiot (6) [258]

8		5		4	

The following is a little naughty because it does not provide us with a specific nesting indicator, using the very general 'with'. However, it redeems itself somewhat by including the word to be nested in the clue itself (which has to go into a word meaning 'finished').

Having finished with me, improved (7) [300]

3		3		1		1

Probably more often than using complete words, we are required to use abbreviations in the nesting game, as demonstrated by:

Try politician for getting into deal (6)

We have to nest MP (an old standby for 'politician') within a word meaning 'deal', namely SALE. This gives us SA(MP)LE = SAMPLE i.e. 'to try'.

In the following, you have to nest 'union leader' (simply U) within something you might buy every day, to get a synonym for 'destitute person'.

Destitute person union leader included daily (6) [089]

12		2		3	

As with other indicators, nesting indicators can be made to look as though they are part of another word, so you must be on the lookout for these. For example in the following, 'inside' is indicating that a component should be nested within the word 'side' itself! (Extra hint: 'left' is standard code for the abbreviation L.)

Walk furtively when left inside (5)   [001]

	6		11	

Finally, although there are a good dozen indicators that crop up regularly (see the table below) you must be on your guard against the ingenuity of compilers in the use of such indicators that might only turn up once in a blue moon. Here are two which use fairly rare nesting indicators. In the first, the indicator is 'Guard' and you are required to nest a word meaning 'long' into a breed of horse.

Long to have the Horse Guard attack (5,4)   [012]

12		4				5		13

In this last one, 'gained possession of' is the nesting indicator and you are required to nest a type of gun into HAS to get a synonym for 'moves fast'.

Has gained possession of the gun and moves fast (7)   [243]

	7		4		5	

NESTING INDICATORS

about	entering	in	round
admitted	getting into	injected	secured
around	has, have	keeps	touring
confining	holding	protects	without

Further nesting clues for practice may be found on page 90.

COMPONENTS — THE BUILDING BLOCKS

The components with which answers are built up in compound and nesting clues consist of groups of letters. The groups will be tend to be short, maybe just one letter, and comprise:

- single letters
- indicated groups of letters
- abbreviations
- colloquialisms
- prefixes
- short or shortish words
- longer words

- short foreign words

- acronyms

- exclamations

- miscellaneous.

Because they provide the compiler with useful combinations for word-building many examples of these components appear quite frequently. Once you get into the swing of regular crosswording, you'll soon become familiar with a wide range. We can't give them all but here are a few to start you off.

SINGLE LETTERS

Often the compiler wishing to use one letter will instruct you to take a letter from a word given in the clue. This can be the first letter and will be indicated by 'first from', 'opener', 'initially' etc., or more subtly by 'a touch of' or 'a hint of'. On the other hand, it can be the last letter of a word, which will be indicated — by 'lastly', 'finally', 'back of' etc. Also, we can be given 'middle of' or 'centre of' where we are required to use the middle letter from an oddly-numbered word. In this way, for example, 'middle of March' signifies R, 'the first of July' clues J, while 'the end of December' clues R. (We look at these in more detail in a later chapter.)

Apart from these, there are many single letters that stand alone in their own right. An old warhorse is L cued by 'learner' or 'inexperienced driver'. Here is an example:

Go by car with an unlicensed driver? Poppycock! (6)

This requires L to be nested within DRIVE ('Go by car') to get DRIVEL.

Some single letters can be indicated by their use in describing shapes. Particularly S-bend, U-bend, T-junction, E-section are common and signalled respectively by 'bend', 'junction' and 'section'. And, of course O which can be signalled by 'duck', 'zero', 'nothing', 'egg', 'circle', 'ring' etc.

Common examples of single letter components are:

caught	C	kilo	K	river	R
circle	O	learner driver	L	round	O
cold	C	loud	F	strong	F
duck	O	nothing	O	time	T
energy	E	page	P	times	X
European	E	power	P	unknown	X,Y, Z
gravity	G	Queen	Q	versus	V
hard	H	quiet	P	zero	O
hot	H	resistance	R		
hydrogen	H	ring	O		

INDICATED GROUPS OF LETTERS

Apart from conventional symbols and letters that we have just examined you can be required to select groups of letters from the clue itself. How this is done will be considered in Chapter 6.

ABBREVIATIONS

Standard abbreviations are part of the armoury, and a versatile fellow is EG which is prompted by 'for example', 'for instance' or 'say', as in the following:

Say lawyer should look up traditional oath (4, Down)

In this instance we have EG ('Say') + AD (DA, 'lawyer' reversed as indicated by 'up') = EGAD, the oath from days of yore. It is a two-way process and, in turn, 'e.g.' (or 'for instance') can signal SAY as in:

Forest god, for instance, putting in time beside river (5)

Here we have two abbreviations from the last section, T for 'time' and R for 'river'. T is nested within SAY ('for instance') and added to R to give SA(T)Y + R = SATYR, a 'forest god'.

Another stock linkage is between 'way' and all its associations as a thoroughfare such as RD, ST, AVE, etc. In the following it calls for ST which has to be linked to a word meaning 'old'.

Put on in the old way first (6) [182]

8		7			1

REP is a common component and is called for with words like 'representative', 'agent' and 'traveller'. In the following it is signalled by 'seller' (with 'off' telling us there is an anagram involved).

Takes back to the seller: the sale's off (7) [274]

		12			11	

One war-horse which refuses to die — it has been around for years and crops up in tabloids and broadsheets alike — is 'good man' for ST (saint). Here it is again (along with an abbreviation for work):

Prevent good man getting work (4)   [014]

8			12

Another popular abbreviation is SS (for steamship, boat, etc). However, there is a regular trick to look out for with this one. The compiler will use a word like 'aboard' meaning that one component (or more) has to be nested **within** SS, in other words you have to put the component 'aboard ship'. The following pulls this stunt.

The trouble aboard is characteristic (7)

The 'characteristic' is TRAIT and has to be nested within SS (i.e. put 'aboard') to give S(TRAIT)S = STRAITS, a synonym for 'trouble'.

Other abbreviations commonly used as components are:

British	B, BR	paid	PD
exercise	PE, PT	race	TT
firm	CO	railway	RLY, RY
mother	MA, MUM, DAM		

COLLOQUIALISMS

Colloquialisms, those words and sounds that we use in speech rather than put down on paper, are frequently drawn upon. For example, MO which we use to signify a short period of time can be signalled by 'moment', 'second' and 'instant'. Also common are elisions between pronouns and verbs, e.g. where in speech 'he had' becomes 'he'd' — which translates as HED in crosswords. Sometimes you have to make the elision yourself; other times you are given it as IM (for I'm) as in the following:

Reckon I'm going into property (8)

In this we are required to nest IM in ESTATE ('property') to get EST(IM)ATE = ESTIMATE.

Some utterances that we all voice but which are unlikely to appear in a dictionary are the signs of hesitation, ER and UM. These are used frequently, for example:

He'll hit the drink with little hesitation! (8)   [015]

9		11			12		

(Hint: you have to lead with a word meaning 'hit'.)

Another couple of ubiquitous colloquialisms are HI (usually signalled by 'greeting') and EH, the sound we might make to emphasise a question. The following uses 'questionable' to call up EH.

Old city number making victory questionable (7)   [144]

5			3		3	

PREFIXES

RE is not a self-standing word but compilers will take advantage of the fact that as a prefix (in 'rebuilt' for example) it has the connotation of 'again'. So they have no qualms in using 'again' as a cue for the two letters as in:

The best dressed again will be in hats (6)

We are given the hint there is anagram by the use of 'dressed'. Then within an anagram of BEST, specifically BETS, we have to nest our RE to get BE(RE)TS = BERETS.

SHORTISH WORDS

There are many short words that conveniently lend themselves as building blocks such as NO, often signalled by 'refusal', as in:

Any refusal to participate would be irksome (5)

where NO is nested within ANY to give AN(NO)Y = ANNOY.

A common short word to be used as a component is AS cued by 'while' or 'when' as in:

Prizes when there's a charge to enter (6)

In this one, WARD ('charge') is 'entered' into AS to give A(WARD)S = AWARDS.

But there are many slightly longer words that are commonly used as components. The following incorporates two regulars (which can be found in the glossary):

Left the pipe outside, but covered (8)   [072]

		12			4		1

Finally in this regard, beware of those innocent little words that look part of the clue and yet are to be incorporated as a component without alteration. In the following, 'any' has that role.

Having to leave, in any case, is an awful pain! (5)   [115]

7		13		

Other short words commonly used as components are:

action	DEED	fish	LING	strange	RUM
advice	TIP	fool	ASS	study	CON
always	ERE, EVER	lair, retreat	DEN	swan	COB, PEN
assume	DON	read	CON	telephone	CALL, RING
badly	ILL	short	SHY	turn	GO
container, vase	URN	soldier	ANT	vicar	REV

LONGER WORDS

Some longer words consist of favourable letter combinations as they stand, for example 'nation' which can be used to build up donation, consternation, ruination and so on. The four common ways of cluing it are 'race', 'people' 'state' or, as in the following, 'country'.

Interested in country accent (10)

With 'Interested in' signalling INTO, we get INTO+NATION = INTONATION.

SHORT FOREIGN WORDS

In this regard it is worth mentioning that compilers do not restrict their use of small words to English. But do not worry too much as they are mainly confined to simple articles and as you proceed you will soon get used to them. The following is interesting in that it requires us to use LE (French for 'the') twice!

French articles about British colony, quite readable (7)

The 'British colony' is GIB which we have to place within LE and LE to get LE(GIB)LE = LEGIBLE.

Common foreign words are:
French   LE, LA, LES, DE, DES, DU, UN, UNE
German   DAS, DER, EIN
Italian   IL
Spanish EL

ACRONYMS

Generally, acronyms are 'words' formed from initial letters such as EU, NATO, UN. Commonly 'peacekeepers' signposts UN, 'drivers' indicates AA or RAC (the driving organisations) and 'non-drinker' TT. There are so many acronyms in the modern world that a complete list cannot be given and you must fall back on your general knowledge. Unfortunately for crossworders, dictionaries and books of lists give the acronym *first*, so you can only use such books if you've got an idea what it looks like.

Very popular are the acronyms for the military services so we have RN for 'navy', RM for 'marine' and RAF for 'fliers'. Also popular are the acronyms for army regiments, the main ones being RA, RE, REME, RO and TA. These may be clued in the general case by 'soldiers' or some description of the nature of the unit such as 'engineers' for RE or 'volunteers' for TA.

Example:

Engineers to be included in team? That's settled (7)

This is quite a neat one in which RE is nested within SQUAD (for 'team') to give SQUA(RE)D = SQUARED (i.e. 'Settled').

EXCLAMATIONS

Exclamations may not be legitimate words but they certainly figure regularly in crossword grids. Popular amongst these are GEE, COR, OW, UGH, WOW and MY. Probably the most popular of all is SH which is cued by words such as 'Silence!' as in:

Heavens! Shot to silence! (4)

where 'Shot' is GO (as in 'have a go') with SH added to yield GOSH. (The compiler is assuming there must be some people left on the planet whose idea of an exclamation is 'Heavens!' or 'Gosh!')

MISCELLANEOUS — THE CLASSICAL WORLD

We mentioned earlier that the use of Roman numerals is common. Specifically we have: I, V, X, L, C, D and M. Compilers also find *combinations* of them useful as components, such as IV, VI, IX, CI etc. The other part of the classical world that is mined for crossword treasures is Greece. Admirable as components and therefore appearing with regularity are Greek letters, the most commonly used being: ETA, MU, NU, XI, PI, RHO, TAU, PHI and CHI.

Checked letters for Chapter 4

1	2	3	4	5	6	7	8	9	10	11	12	13
D	U	E	T	N	I	A	S	W	K	L	P	O

Chapter 5

OTHER TYPES OF CLUE

DOUBLE DEFINITION

This type of clue consists of **two** words (or phrases) which are both synonyms for another word (or phrase) which is the answer. In this way for example, 'signify' and 'average' are linked and lead to MEAN. The clue comes in two forms. Firstly, there is the kind where two concepts are placed side by side with no indicators. Example:

Blue feathers (4)

This is quite straightforward. We have two definitions and the word they share in meaning is DOWN. The next two are just as straightforward.

Rapid diet (4)   [292]

1		2	

Get hold of some eggs (6)   [071]

	3				4

In these the setter often aims to disguise the double definition by constructing the clue in such a way that it looks like a single definition of which the following is a good example:

Colour blind (5)

The answer being SHADE.

The second form of the clue is where the setter interposes something between the two concepts. This something can be a word, a phrase or an item of punctuation and has the function of linking (or separating) the two. The most common is their being linked by 'and', as in:

Commercial house and stable (4)

where the answer is FIRM.

Or the two concepts can be shown to be equivalent by using words such as 'is' or 'being' as in:

Angry at being anaesthetised (3,3)

for which the answer is PUT OUT. With practice you can take these interposed words as indicators that you have a double definition clue on your hands. Once you have identified the indicator and its purpose, it is useful then to ignore it, as you might ignore 'when you' in solving the following.

Come to light, when you arrive (4,2)   [016]

5		6			7

The following is a summary of indicators that you will come across:

Notion	Examples of Double Definition Indicators	Example of clue	Answer
Linkages	and, to, for, with, as, so	Remain and support? (4)	STAY
Separation	comma (,) long dash (—)	Gave a caning — exhausted! (7)	WHACKED
One producing the other	produces, makes, provides, gives, shows, from, that, by	Competitors making records (7)	ENTRIES
Equivalence	is, are, being, in, to appear	Wash is what I do when the alarm goes off (4)	WAKE
Existing	together where, with, when, whilst, in which	Finish with remnant (3)	END
Belonging	of, having, apostrophe (')	Nelson's powerful position? (10)	STRONGHOLD
Contradiction	but, or, though, question mark (?)	Complain, though it's for one's own protection (4)	RAIL

The clues so far use relatively short words but you can expect long words just as often. They can make you think too, as the next one probably will. (To identify the two separate definitions in the clue, ignore 'by'.)

Causing worry by cancelling payment of bill? (10)   [145]

8		2		5		3			9

It is suggested that you remember the answer to the following because, when you continue doing crosswords after working through this book, it won't be long before you see its solution making an appearance elsewhere.

Steal fitting (11)   [267]

	10		6			6			5	

And now, an even longer example, a clever one with a touch of whimsy about it (hint: ignore 'on'):

Fussing about trivial details on parting (4-9)   [234]

4			6	2		3			5			9

The following is a double definition type that employs a trick that we have not considered before.

Contraption that will banish evil? (6)

The answer to this is DEVICE which obviously fits 'contraption', the first definition. However, the second definition 'banish evil' expects us to think of DE-VICE, a word that is not in the English language! Such a word is described as a **coined word**. Also known as **coinages**, these are existing prefixes and words which are given a new meaning by the compiler. In the use of coinages, the rules of the language are followed so the new meaning is quite legitimate; it is just that the word is simply not used that way by the general populace. Quite a few have become standard in crosswords and one of the most common is 'detail'. This uses the prefix DE- in the same manner as 'de-vice' above and compilers use it as a synonym for 'to cut the tail off'. With this meaning, 'detail' and 'detailed' come in very handy for compilers when they aim to cut the end letter from a word. In the same vein there's 'design' — to take one's name off a document. Other examples are 'missed' as an adjective for an unmarried woman, together with its opposite 'not missed' to describe a married woman. In this way, when the adjectives 'booked' or 'titled' appear in association with a person (such as 'titled gentleman') they can mean the person's name is in the title of a well-known **book**. The following embodies a regular coinage so, when you have solved it, it could be worth remembering. (Hint: think how one could describe a particular domestic article which is 'liable to get lit up'.)

Liable to get lit up, which is bad (6)   [215]

11					12

Finally, the double definition type of clue will occasionally use what are called **heteronyms**. These are 'different' words identical in spelling but distinct in sound and meaning. For example if WOUND is pronounced one way it has the meaning of 'turned', while pronounced another way it means 'injury' or 'to injure'. The following makes use of a very common heteronym.

Metal guide (4) [111]

3			12

The next is also a crossword regular but in this case it has been camouflaged by the choice of the clue's first word. (Two hints: ignore 'as a' and remember that 'register' can signify a *musical* register.)

Register as a fish (4) [286]

			2

Sometimes the difference in pronunciation can be so slight with the passage of time as to be now almost non-existent, as in:

Meaning it is from abroad? (6) [177]

		10		6	

Checked letters for DOUBLE DEFINITIONS

1	2	3	4	5	6	7	8	9	10	11	12
F	S	L	H	T	R	P	U	G	P	W	D

SINGLE DEFINITION

This is a fairly common clue in tabloid puzzles but is probably a little rarer in the broadsheets. It is characterized by masquerading as a clue from a 'quick' crossword, giving what appears to be a straightforward definition, usually consisting of two words. Unlike most cryptic clues there is no secondary information given, so, for it to justify its position in a cryptic, there must be some kind of twist. Example:

Growing nippers (8)

The uninitiated might immediately come up with CHILDREN. It looks OK — it fits the definition and has the right number of letters. However, one should realise that both words in the clue have been chosen specially and CHILDREN, while looking right superficially, does not embody any deception. So we should feel uneasy about our first stab at the answer; and we would be justified in feeling uneasy because the answer is in fact TEETHING. The problem with these apparently simple clues is that even a seasoned solver cannot be sure of the answer until he or she has a few checked letters in place (breaking Rule 3 on page 15 but complying with Rule 4!).

The justification for inclusion of such a clue in a cryptic may be no more than there is an attempt to divert our attention, as in:

Used in scullery (3)

where the answer is OAR. These next two have equal simplicity:

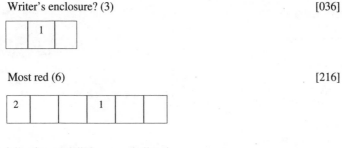

Writer's enclosure? (3)   [036]

Most red (6)   [216]

The following are a little more challenging:

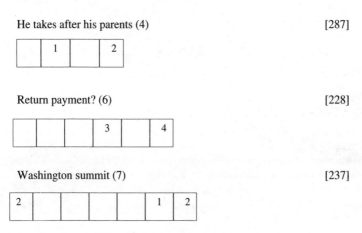

He takes after his parents (4)   [287]

Return payment? (6)   [228]

Washington summit (7)   [237]

The following embodies a clever use of the words 'He's said to'. To crack it you've got to forget its everyday meaning of 'he is believed to'.

He's said to end conversation (5)   [087]

		5		2

The next example is very neat — it is short but quite clever in presenting you with a scenario that has nothing to do with the answer. So forget telephones.

An outside line to ring (7)   [188]

	6		5			

Like the double-definition clue, the single definition type provides an arena for the deployment of **coined words**. (We came across an example of this in the earlier section where DE-VICE had the meaning of 'banish evil'.) A contender for the most common coinage of all is 'soundly', which appears even more frequently in homophone clues but here makes an appearance in a single definition. Under 'soundly' your dictionary will only give meanings with the sense of 'securely' but there is no logical reason why it shouldn't mean 'noisily'. With this coined meaning, the following can only have one answer.

Sleep soundly? (5)   [136]

	7			

In the following, 'quivered' is a coinage. Think about it!

One quivered, perhaps, when bowing (6)   [103]

6		8			

Nor will your dictionary carry the meaning given to 'provisional' as it is used in the following; but it is quite justified.

Make provisional arrangements (5)   [268]

	6		1	

Checked letters for SINGLE DEFINITIONS

1	2	3	4	5	6	7	8
E	R	S	M	G	A	N	C

DOUBLE DUTY (or the '& lit.' clue)

The double duty clue is one where part or the whole of the clue has two functions and so has to be read and interpreted twice. For example, in the following:

Cabaret astonishes who? (5,4)

the word 'astonishes' serves two purposes. Firstly, it is an anagram indicator targeting 'who' which we have to re-jig into HOW. Secondly, it is a synonym calling up FLOORS (with the meaning of 'astonishes' i.e. figuratively 'knocks out'). Putting the two components together we get FLOORS/HOW which we split appropriately to get the answer: FLOOR SHOW, a synonym for 'cabaret'.

Similarly in the next one, the first part of the clue has two meanings.

'Man in Lead Collapses' for instance (8)

'Man in Lead Collapses' is simultaneously an **instruction** for getting the answer while at the same time being an **example** of the answer. 'Collapses' tells us we have an anagram of IN LEAD, so we have HE ('Man') + ADLINE = HEADLINE — which the phrase 'Man in Lead Collapses' could be in a newspaper!

However, the double-duty clue comes into its own when the **whole** clue has two functions. For this reason it is also called the '**and lit**' clue because, having read the clue once to identify the instructions, you have to read the whole thing again, this time **literally**, in order to get the definition. The following is a fully-fledged 'double duty':

A torque of sorts all round the world (7)

From a first reading we might rightly identify 'of sorts' as an anagram indicator and note that 'A torque' provides us with the requisite seven letters. Shuffling these, we come up with EQUATOR. Now, one of the meanings of 'torque' is necklace so when we read the whole clue **again** we have 'a necklace of sorts all round the world' — which confirms that with EQUATOR we have the right answer.

So, the pure double duty clue is **simultaneously** the definition **and** the set of instructions for finding the answer. From the compiler's point of view, this constraint makes it a difficult clue to construct and it is thus quite a rare breed. It also puts an onus on the solver who has to read and interpret the clue twice. Many 'double duty' clues are relatively easy and are often included for our enjoyment rather than as a mind-boggling challenge.

The next one is a little awkward in appearance but it no doubt gave satisfaction to its compiler as it certainly provides satisfaction when we work out why our solution is correct.

First parent (either) (4)

A first reading of the clue suggests ADAM or EVE, and on that basis we would plump for ADAM — if for no other reason than EVE doesn't have the requisite number of letters. But we have to read it again to understand the significance of the word 'either'. Then we might realise that the clue **does** cover EVE — for she can be described as A DAM (i.e. a mother)! Now that's clever.

Here are some for you to try and remember to read them twice.

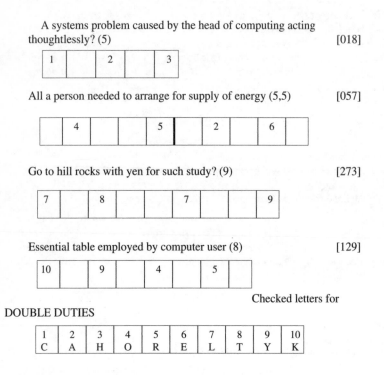

A systems problem caused by the head of computing acting thoughtlessly? (5)   [018]

1		2		3

All a person needed to arrange for supply of energy (5,5)   [057]

	4			5		2		6	

Go to hill rocks with yen for such study? (9)   [273]

7		8			7			9

Essential table employed by computer user (8)   [129]

10		9		4		5	

Checked letters for

DOUBLE DUTIES

1	2	3	4	5	6	7	8	9	10
C	A	H	O	R	E	L	T	Y	K

THE WHIMSICAL CLUE

This contains only a definition and nothing else, the definition being based on some kind of pun. (Also called the '**cryptic definition**' type; but the label 'whimsical' has the virtue of embodying the notion of a caprice or playfulness — as in music a caprice is a playful work of art — and playfulness is what puns are all about!) In these, a phrase or sentence is given very often with a question mark signalling that the answer is related to it in some quirky or humorous way. Of the different types of clue, this is the one where reference books are of the least use because, with no indicators or other conventional help, the field is wide open. All you can do is try to tap into the way the compiler is thinking. Example:

It's just one drink after another! (6)

for which the answer is CHASER. This type of clue can be quite a stumbling block in the completion of a grid and is thankfully restricted in use, although they do provide satisfaction and maybe a chuckle when cracked. And now some 'whimsicals' for you.

Temporary means to stop part of clutch overheating (3-5)   [078]

	1				2		3	

Jam session? (4,4)   [183]

4		5			6		4

His enemies got fatally jarred (3,4)   [175]

	7		8		8	

Biblical figure associated with ducking the issue? (4,3,7)   [227]

	6					3						5	

Checked letters for WHIMSICALS

1	2	3	4	5	6	7	8
G	I	E	R	S	O	L	B

We are now in a position to summarise the different kinds of clue and their constituents:

	CONSTITUENTS			
	Definition	Definition	One Instruction (or indicator)	Several instructions (or indicators)
Standard cryptic — simple	•		•	
Standard cryptic — compound	•		•	•
Single definition	•			
Double definition	•	•	(possibly)	
Double Duty	•		(masked)	
Whimsical	•			

Chapter 6

MORE ON THE SELECTION OF LETTERS

You may have come across riddles consisting of short poems where the first letter of each line makes up the answer. In this form it is an ancient puzzle known as an acrostic — from the Greek, AKROS (tip) + STIKHOS (line of verse). The acrostic principle is given new life in the modern crossword and appears in several disguises.

FIRST LETTERS

Consider:

Sensational opening line used regularly in debates (5)

Here the acrostic is being presented in its classical form where **all** first letters are used. 'Sensational' is our definition while 'opening' tells us we are to use the first letters of the words that follow to get the answer LURID. (In fact, the acrostic can be seen as a special case of the compound clue where only letters are components.)

Or, as we have seen before, you can be required to use only the initial letter of one word in the clue, as in:

Cheerful young male worker takes in union leader (7)

The 'union leader' is U which is nested in BOY ('young male') to be followed by ANT ('worker') giving BUOYANT, cheerful.

LAST LETTERS

Or you may have to use the end letters from a sequence of words as in:

At last Nigel came — and went first! (3)

Here, 'last' is telling us to use the last letters of the words that follow it. So we have LED, which satisfies the definition 'went first'. More commonly we can be required to use only one last letter. Example:

Colonist feeding dog with last of offal (7)

The 'last of offal' is L which has to be inserted (i.e. fed) into SETTER ('dog') to give the answer SETTLER, a 'colonist'. One devious little trick to look out for in this regard is when the indicator of first or last letter is disguised as **part of** the word itself. Hence, Minehead clues M, Gravesend clues S and so on. For example, until you are aware of the device being used, the following could be difficult.

Dunderhead joining a union and hanging around (9)

Here 'Dunderhead' signifies D which, along with 'union' calling up ALLIANCE, gives us D+ALLIANCE = DALLIANCE (i.e. dallying or 'hanging around.). Very often, both the first and last letter ploys are used in the same clue. That first and last letters are to be selected will be indicated by a phrase such as 'extremes of'. In the following, 'extremely' has the same function.

Arrive extremely dirty — it makes you laugh (6)

'Arrive' calls for COME while 'extremely dirty' clues DY to give us COME+DY = COMEDY. Finally, bear in mind that occasionally the indicators discussed above ('start of', 'end of' etc.) can also signify that we have to borrow **two** letters.

INTERMEDIATE LETTERS — THE MIDDLE

Moreover, **other** letters from a given word can be selected for use. You can be required to select the middle letter of a word, as in:

Polytheistic composer missing in centre of China (5)

This is quite difficult because there are a lot of composers to pick from. With some thought, we may see that PAGANINI fits the bill as the 'composer' from which we have to omit two elements: IN (word in clue) and I (the 'centre of China'). This gives PAGAN, 'polytheistic'. Just as 'first' and 'last' can require two letters, so can 'centre' and 'middle'. And the trick will be employed quite cleverly; for example, 'middle of June' is often a cue for UN.

INTERMEDIATE LETTERS — ODDS AND EVENS

The other popular letter selections are where we have to single out odd or even letters in a sequence. Starting with odd letters:

Twitch, having taken the odds (3)

This is quite easy but smart too, as the compiler has noticed that the odd letters of 'twitch' give a synonym for the same word! Hence, the answer — TIC.

In the following, the word 'regularly' signifies the choosing of even letters:

Actor's words regularly delivered by McQueen? (3)

where the solution CUE is the sequence of *even* letters in 'McQueen'.

INTERMEDIATE LETTERS — MISCELLANEOUS

You can be required to extract a **specifically** numbered letter from an associated word and this trick can come in a variety of forms: 'fourth of July' clues Y, 'Beethoven's Fifth' H, 'The Third Man' N, 'November the Fifth' M, 'a close second' L and so on. Notice how obvious these are when you look at them in isolation and know what you are looking for — but when situated in a well-written clue they can add to the confusion.

Here are some for you to try that play the same tricks.

Originally all my pupils heard ode read, on a Grecian urn (7)   [013]

1		2		3		1

Points to an oddly shaped bread (5)   [189]

2		4		1

Region by borders of Arimathea (4)   [289]

	5		1

Austrian scientist, first among many (but less superior) (4)   [193]

	1		6

The animal came a close second (5)   [311]

	1			7

Checked letters

1	2	3	4	5	6	7
A	P	O	T	R	H	L

Examples of letter indicators:

FIRST	MIDDLE	LAST	ODDS & EVENS
at first	central	at last	odds
leading character in	centre of	base of	oddly
opening of	heart of	foot of	even
originally	middle of	lastly	regularly

Chapter 7

COMPLICATIONS SET IN

Now's the time to step up a gear. When we first looked at the basic tricks and the types of clue in which they are employed we restricted ourselves wherever possible to simple examples — simple in the sense that only one gimmick was used at a time. In actual grids you will certainly find clues characterised by this kind of simplicity but clues in the main will go beyond these limitations.

In fact, clues may be complicated in at least four ways:

> 1. The compound clue can have more than two elements.
>
> 2. More than one gimmick can be employed in any one clue.
>
> 3. Difficult vocabulary can be used, or the links between synonyms can be tenuous — the dreaded sleeper.
>
> 4. The definition can be made difficult to identify.

Let us look at each of these in turn.

THE MULTI-COMPONENT COMPOUND CLUE

You will recall that in this kind of clue we are required to put components together to arrive at the answer. As a reminder that this can be complicated merely by having many components we shall look at a couple made up of five building blocks.

The rogue produces a right when caught with a left (6)

This is quite straightforward as the five bits it embodies are only short words and abbreviations, without any devious manipulation in their use. 'Rogue' is our target which we achieve by amalgamating the parts in the sequence in which they are presented to us: R ('right') + AS ('when') + C ('caught') + A + L ('left') = RASCAL.

The following five-parter is equally straightforward.

English duke provided one church building (7)   [081]

1		2			3	

THE USE OF MORE THAN ONE GIMMICK

Typically, the setter will try to trip us up by using two or more tricks in one clue. So we can have an anagram embodying a letter indicator, a nesting clue embodying an anagram and so on. In fact, any combination of the tricks we have looked at earlier. Let us start with the easiest — the run.

THE RUN

A common complication for this fellow is that the letters of the run should be laid before us in reverse order as in:

Relaxed and turned in because so old (5)

Reading the clue backwards you shouldn't have much trouble finding the answer LOOSE which satisfies the definition of 'Relaxed'. Can you spot the reverse run in the following?

Dog going up in big rocket (5 DOWN[1])   [252]

		4		2

ANAGRAMS

One way that the anagram can be made more complicated is by providing us with a large number of words or components, which have to be manipulated. The solution to the following monster lies in an anagram of **five** constituents (one a letter while the others are words present in the clue).

Egotistical in the extreme, if ideas not open to change? (4-11)   [133]

5		6			7		8			8		9		

A further complication with the anagram is that it may be mixed up with the notion of omission — so that we may be required to omit a letter or two before we even start our shuffling. For instance, in the following the 'leader of Cuba' has to be 'sacked'.

Criticise Castro, wanting leader of Cuba sacked (5)

In uncoded language, we have to omit C ('leader of Cuba') before we re-arrange 'Castro' into a word meaning 'criticise', i.e. ROAST.

The next one requires you to omit **two** letters from one of the words before you can jumble up the remaining letters to find a synonym equivalent to 'light'.

---

[1] Remember the significance of the code word 'up' as a reversal indicator in a down clue (Chapter 3).

Make light of being a bit lame with a broken leg (5)   [021]

10		1		11	

Anagrams can be used in combination with any of the other devices and we will look at some of these later, but let us finish this section by seeing how the anagram can be used with other letter indicators. The following is reasonably difficult because, apart from the added complication of a letter indicator, there is a bit of a 'sleeper' aspect to the definition's link with the answer. (The link is completely legitimate but, as it is an example rather than a straight synonym, it is not the first word you would think of.)

Health risks from strategic exchange, initially out of control (10)

Despite the presence of an anagram indicator ('out of control'), it is not immediately obvious how to go about solving it because the phrase 'strategic exchange' hangs together so well that we might be loath to break it up. Here goes. The letter indicator is 'initially' and we are looking for a synonym for, or better still an example of, 'Health risks'. This is arrived at as an anagram of STRATEGIC + E ('exchange initially') = CIGARETTES. A satisfying answer but, you might agree, not the easiest of clues.

The next anagram, in which the letter indicator is 'front of' and the anagram indicator is 'damaged', is a shade easier:

Not reacting as front of precious vase is damaged (7)   [235]

7		5			12	

THE HOMOPHONE

By its nature the homophone is more restricted than other devices in its capability of being related to other tricks. Consequently, when the setter seeks to complicate the issue using a homophone, he usually can only pair it up with a compound clue or, as in the following, the nesting device.

When in the Palladium, Raymond is spoken well of (7)

'Spoken' is a standard indicator telling us we have a homophone. The homophone element in the clue is 'Raymond is' which we translate as RAISE (i.e. Ray's). Then, nesting RAISE within PD (symbol for the chemical element palladium), we get PRAISED. Note here that 'spoken' is doing double duty as the homophone indicator **and** as part of the definition 'spoken well of'.

In the following, a sound-alike for 'Swindled' is nested within a synonym for 'cunning' to achieve the solution.

Swindled, we hear, taken in by cunning? Absolutely (8)   [255]

5		4			9		

OMISSION

Omission can be used to make clues more difficult by being employed in conjunction with several other devices and clue types. Here it is part of a compound clue:

Passionate Eastern ruler loses article on railway (6)

The 'Eastern ruler' in question is SULTAN from which we lose the article AN. To get to the definition ('Passionate') we add the remaining four letters to RY for 'railway' so: SULT + RY = SULTRY.

In the following you have to omit **four** letters from a word and construct the answer as a straightforward compound.

Camera came out with the others — that's most unusual (6)   [216]

4			1		9

REVERSALS

Apart from with the run, the reversal idea works very well in conjunction with compound clues.

Pet takes the wrong turning at a medium pace (7)

'Pet' is DOG. Easy enough. 'Turning' tells us we have a reversal which we have to apply to TORT (i.e. a legal term for 'wrong'). Putting them together we get DOG + TROT = DOGTROT, 'a medium pace'.

In the following two-part compound clue, 'backing' is the reverse indicator. If you have trouble, look up 'gunmen' and 'challenger' in the glossary.

Advent of gunmen backing challenger (7)   [288]

13		4		12		6

Sometimes **all** the elements in a compound clue may have to be reversed.

Minor disturbance setting foreign capital right back (6)

Here we have ROME ('foreign capital') + RT (abbreviation for 'right'). We know we have a reversal because of the presence of 'back' so, reversing the lot, we arrive at TREMOR, a 'minor disturbance'.

The following compound clue is ingeniously put together. Like the previous example, it consists of two elements, both of which have to be reversed.

Bolshevik turned up by 9.50 (5)   [091]

6		8		8

Finally, the following is also a neatly constructed compound where **three** elements are reversed, while the elements themselves are to be in reverse order.

Peron woman's reverend father turns up first, producing opposition (11)

[310]

13		12		4		13	9		12	

NESTING

As anything can be nested within anything else, this device must be almost as universal as the anagram.

COMPLETE WORD		COMPLETE WORD
WORD WITH OMISSION	any of these can be nested within any of these	WORD WITH OMISSION
RUN		RUN
ANAGRAM		ANAGRAM
HOMOPHONE		HOMOPHONE
REVERSAL		REVERSAL

Even though the above schema is not necessarily the full story, it alone gives 49 possible permutations! From this you can see why we can't give examples of them all, but here are a few nesting combinations.

In the following, a complete unadulterated word is nested within an anagram.

First there's noise: a gale blowing outside (7)

The definition is 'First', 'blowing' is an anagram indicator and 'outside' is a nesting indicator. So we nest DIN ('noise') within an anagram of GALE to get LEA(DIN)G = LEADING.

Your practice example does the same: an unaltered word (synonym of 'expert') is to be nested within an anagram of 'loss'. ('Silly' tells us that an anagram is involved.)

Soothes expert involved in silly loss (7) [269]

5		6		3		5

Alternatively, an anagram can be nested within an unaltered word, as in:

Kidnap though poor Bud was caught in act (6)

'Poor Bud' signifies an anagram of BUD while 'caught in' denotes that we have to nest it within ACT to get a word meaning 'kidnap'. Hence we get A(BDU)CT = ABDUCT.

Similarly, in the next one you have to nest an anagram of SLIM within a word meaning 'survey' to get a 'shipping line'.

Survey encompassing slim new shipping line (8) [187]

7		2		5		6	

Stepping up another gear, the following practice clue embodies **four** tricks, specifically:

> nesting — as indicated by 'in'
>
> reversal — as indicated by 'up' (possible meaning in a DOWN clue) omission — as indicated by 'not'
>
> and an abbreviation — which is a standard abbreviation so we are not told about it.

Turn up in revue, not concerned with fashion (5, Down) [198]

12		10		1

Nesting can be made more involved by requiring us to nest more than one component. Consider:

Power state invested in magistrate to give pardon (8)

'Invested in' tells us it is a nesting type clue. The two components to be inserted are 'Power state' which are respectively P (for 'power') and RI (for the state of Rhode Island'). These are slipped into REEVE, an old word for 'magistrate'[2]. Thus RE(P + RI)EVE = REPRIEVE, 'pardon'. Try the following.

Frenchman getting on fine in south-eastern Havana? (5)   [293]

	11		14	

(Hint: the two components to be nested are an abbreviation for Frenchman along with a synonym for 'fine', both of which are to go into 'south-eastern'. But look out because you have sleeper on your hands, inasmuch as you have been given an *example* of what is required rather than a *direct* synonym.)

Finally, let us look at a case of three components being nested.

A couple of models in the circle changing sides (7)

'Model' is often code for T (as in a Ford Model T) so here 'a couple of models' is simply A+T+T = ATT. This has to be nested in a word meaning 'circle' i.e. RING, so we get R(ATT)ING which is a way of describing the activity of 'changing sides'! Your practice example is:

Road I left to enter river slowly (7)   [259]

9		4		2		

(Hint: you need the name of a river into which you nest three separate components covered by 'Road I left' to give you 'slowly'.)

COMPLICATIONS WITH DEFINITIONS

The compiler has an obligation to provide a definition. On the other hand, he is under no obligation to make it clear; in fact, he will often go out of his way to make it as clear as mud. In passing we have seen examples of this being done already but let's summarise by considering the ways he can avoid giving us a straightforward definition. These include:

  • the abstruse synonym

[2] A word which may be familiar to us if we are lawyers, have read 'The Canterbury Tales' or have simply done a few crosswords!

- the disguised definition
- definition by characteristic
- definition by function
- definition by example.

THE ABSTRUSE SYNONYM

This is our friend the sleeper again — this time in an extreme form. Take the following.

Reported decline of togetherness? (5)

On the surface this looks easy enough — it is a short clue with a short answer, a mere five letters. However, the compiler has picked an abstruse synonym for us to grapple with and we probably couldn't get near cracking it until we have some letters in place. The definition is 'togetherness' and the answer is arrived at via the homophone SINK ('reported decline') to give us SYNCH. All very well because 'synch' as a synonym for 'togetherness' is quite legitimate — but it is a fairly difficult notion for us to hit on out of the blue. Firstly, as an abbreviation of synchronization, it is a colloquialism rather than a formal word. Such terms, unless we are given some guidance in the clue, are always difficult to think of. Secondly, it is a very distant synonym in the sense that the OED, for instance, does not actually *use* the word 'together' or 'togetherness' in its definition of the word; while the writer's thesaurus doesn't give the term at all. So we are entirely on our own in coming up with the word, despite the fact that we would have to acknowledge that it is quite valid. Lesson: be on the lookout for 'off the map' synonyms!

THE DISGUISED DEFINITION

The compiler can make it difficult for you to identify the definition. Take the following:

Where one golfer differs from another (8)

If you begin at the beginning and concentrate on the possibility of 'Where' being the definition, you might start considering the various terms for parts of a golf course. With no luck from that quarter you might cast further afield to thinking of the names of specific courses. On the other hand, 'another' might be the definition. All on the wrong track. The definition is the *whole* clue. The *stance* of a golfer is *one* instance of how he differs from another golfer. To arrive at the solution we read IN STANCE as one word to give us — INSTANCE. Devious!

Another way of disguising the definition is by breaking it up with unnecessary punctuation — see the beginning of the next chapter.

DEFINITION BY CHARACTERISTIC

Rather than provide us with a synonym as a dictionary-style definition, the compiler often merely mentions one of the features of the thing that we are looking for, as in the following.

Taking money out with security number? There's a point to it (7-3)

'Taking money out' is DRAWING and 'security number' is PIN. Putting them together we get the answer: DRAWING-PIN. But note, the compiler has not actually defined drawing pin in a straightforward way; he has simply told us that we are looking for something that has a point!

DEFINITION BY FUNCTION

Another ploy of the compiler is not to give a direct definition but to give one of its functions. For example the nearest one can get to classifying the following is as a double definition type, although there is only one clear definition.

Dash — for coal (7)

'Dash' suggests we are looking for something meaning to 'run quickly' and indeed we are because the answer is SCUTTLE. However, in fairness, for 'scuttle' to be fully synonymous with the second definition we really need something like 'a receptacle for carrying coal' — but we have to be satisfied with 'for coal' which is merely a description of a scuttle's function.

DEFINITION BY EXAMPLE

It is a convention of the crossword game that the definition may be in the form of an example and this will usually be signalled by cues such as 'perhaps', 'for instance', 'for example', 'say'. Consider:

Eccentric banker's an inhabitant of Lincoln, perhaps (9)

The definition here is 'inhabitant of Lincoln, perhaps', so that is what we are looking for: an example of what could be described as 'an inhabitant of Lincoln'. As far as instructions go we have 'Eccentric' which suggests we have an anagram on our hands. Well, if we are not American we may have to refer to our atlas to discover that Lincoln is the capital of Nebraska, but if we merely shuffle the letters of 'banker's an' we duly get NEBRASKAN and we have the answer. To use an example as the definition in this way is common practice and quite acceptable because we have an *alternative* means of getting at the answer through the instructions — which is a cornerstone of the cryptic.

However, the compiler can stretch the convention to the limit and give us *nothing but examples*, as in the following case.

Dogs, for example, or man with capital? (4)

Here we have no instructions as to how to construct the solution and our only guide consists of **two** examples! Is this legitimate? In its defence it could be said that the ploy is excusable on the grounds that: 1. it is not too difficult, the answer being ISLE (Isle of Dogs, Isle of Man); and 2. there is a cryptic aspect to the phrase 'man with capital', i.e. a capital letter: Man. An enjoyable clue to solve, but devious. So look out for tricks being played with definitions.

For your part, you might find a problem simply identifying the definitions in the following.

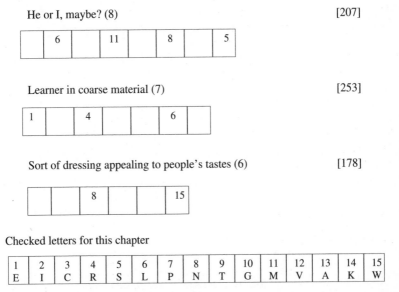

He or I, maybe? (8)   [207]

	6		11		8		5

Learner in coarse material (7)   [253]

1		4			6	

Sort of dressing appealing to people's tastes (6)   [178]

		8			15

Checked letters for this chapter

1	2	3	4	5	6	7	8	9	10	11	12	13	14	15
E	I	C	R	S	L	P	N	T	G	M	V	A	K	W

Chapter 8

SUBSIDIARY TRICKS

THE STUTTERED OPENING

Unexpected double letters at the beginning of a word (giving the appearance of a stutter) are reasonably common and can mean a variety of things. The simplest interpretation is to see the 'stuttered' letter merely as a single letter indicator, as is the intention in the following:

Standard to f-fall behind? (4)

Here we have to ignore the hyphen and simply treat the first F as a separate component to make up the answer. 'Fall behind' clues LAG so we have F+LAG giving us FLAG which is the required 'standard'. But it can get more complicated. Witness the following:

Have the means to pay for a M-Mondeo? (6)

Here the double-M means that we have to think of a synonym for Mondeo, then double its first letter! If you are a car person you will know a Mondeo is a Ford i.e. A FORD. Doubling the 'F' we get A-F-FORD = AFFORD = 'have the means to pay'.

IGNORANCE IS BLISS

We have already seen where we are obliged to ignore some part of the sentence in order to make sense of what's required. For example, in the following run-type clue

It may indicate disinterest in Welsh Rugby (5)

we have to ignore the space between the last two words or we'll have trouble identifying the answer: SHRUG.

Moreover, when in doubt, we should ignore the following too: brackets, quotation marks, full stops, commas, apostrophes, hyphens, colons and assorted dashes. They are often inserted to break links between words or concepts, links which you need to retain to get to your answer. One of the most common devices in crosswords is 'I've' to clue IVE where we have to ignore the apostrophe, as in:

Sixties hairstyle I've given to one working hard (7)

Here BEE ('one working') + H('hard') + IVE('I've') leads to BEEHIVE, a 'sixties hairstyle'.

Then there's the comma that gets in the way:

In speech, giant is tense (7)

What this is asking for is a word for 'giant' which is a sound-alike for the answer. The stepping-stone word is TITAN but the placing of the comma nudges us to look for some kind of sense in 'giant is tense'. The comma subtly tries to break the flow that leads us to the sound-alike answer TIGHTEN.

In the following compound clue you must ignore both the apostrophe and the comma.

Wife's needed little time, cooking apple (7)

This is quite clever on the part of the compiler because, if you read the comma at face value, you will be led to the suggestion that the definition is a specific 'cooking apple' (and you may not know the names of too many cooking apples) while simultaneously being denied the last component in making up the actual solution. With the apostrophe and comma ignored, the answer is built up in the following way: RIB ('Wife') + S (i.e. 's) + T ('time') + ON ('cooking') to give RIBSTON, which is a kind of apple (and *not* necessarily a cooking apple).

The question mark can be similarly intrusive:

State of course? Very keen on making investigation (5,4)

The gap in this example should be between 'on' and 'making' because the first six words have to be thought of *together*. Ignoring the question mark which has been slipped in to throw us, we come up with GOING('State of course' in racing) + INTO ('Very keen on') to give us GOING INTO, 'making investigation'.

The following is a compound clue but we are encouraged to think otherwise by the long dash breaking up the components:

Making further use of troops — using manpower (9)

If there's to be a break it should be after 'of' because the definition consists of the first four words. 'Troops' (RE) belongs with 'using manpower' (CYCLING) to give us RECYCLING i.e. 'making further use of'. In the next one, the same punctuation mark is used to break up an anagram.

Terrible nag — folk banned The Old Lady (4,2,7)

'Nag' needs to be used alongside 'folk' but the two words have been separated by a long dash. Knowing that it is an anagram (the use of 'Terrible' tells us that), see if you can solve the clue if the punctuation is replaced by what we might call natural breaks:

Terrible — nag folk banned — The Old Lady (4,2,7)   [270]

1		2		3			2		4		2	

The dash is also used to break the natural flow in the following:

Bird around north — no hedge sparrow (7)

Given that north is N and that two components have to be nested within a complete word, see if you can now solve the clue if the natural links and breaks are inserted:

Bird around 'north no' — hedge sparrow (7)   [161]

5		2		3		

In the next one, the brackets are the villains:

Doctor (university lecturer) taken aboard by firm (10)

They are inserted in such a way as to suggest that 'university lecturer' is a description of 'Doctor' when in fact they apply to the latter part of the clue. 'University lecturer' is UL and has to be nested within CONSTANT (i.e. firm) to give CONS(UL)TANT = CONSULTANT meeting the definition 'Doctor'.

FALSE LINKAGES BREAKING THE CHAIN

In stage magic, the term 'force' is used to describe what the conjuror does when he ensures that you select the card he wants you to select — without you realising it. Similarly, the wily setter can 'force' us to see connections where they don't exist. One way of doing this is by choosing words and placing them in such a way that our brain automatically sees them as linked. The following is an admirable clue to demonstrate this point because, not only is it subtly constructed, it plays the same trick *twice*, so some time can pass before we work out what the clue is about.

Not very smart, eating the anticoagulant (7)

Our first inclination is to see either 'Not very smart' or 'anticoagulant' as the definition. Neither is. And neither are what they seem to be! The first stumbling block is that it is very difficult for us *not* to see the first three words as running together. 'Not very smart' is a natural combination of words making its own sense. However, we have to break them down to give us the true definition that we have to aim for — 'Not very'. Secondly, it is difficult for us to realise that the two sections of 'anticoagulant' also need to be separated. Once we have cottoned on to this, the answer is achieved as follows. 'Coagulant' is being used as an anagram indicator — we did tell you setters can be very ingenious in this regard — requiring the letters ANTI to be re-shuffled. 'Eating' is a nesting indicator and we have to nest the re-sorted letters AINT within a word meaning 'smart', FLY. This materialises as F(AINT)LY which meets the definition of 'not very' in the form of FAINTLY.

In a similar fashion, hyphens can be used to suggest there is a link *between* two words where there isn't one. In the following clue the words 'bath' and 'time' are linked in this way but have to be treated separately.

'Watch with Mother' interrupts bath-time negotiator (8)

'Watch with Mother' is LO ('Watch') + MA ('Mother') = LOMA which then has to be nested between DIP('bath') and T('time') to give DIP(LOMA)T = DIPLOMAT, a 'negotiator'.

Less complicated is the following, which plays the same trick. By inserting a hyphen in 'whip-round', we are being encouraged to think of the term to mean a form of subscription.

Whip-round for old statesman (4)   [185]

	6		3

In fact, the clue is a simple compound clue made up of 'whip' and 'round' which have to be treated as **separate** components. The definition is 'old statesman' and you have to think of a self-standing word meaning 'whip' to which you add a symbol for 'round' to get the answer.

False links can be used to mislead you by simple choice of words. In the following the words 'walk back' have been carefully placed to make you read them as together.

On the walk back will carry it (8)   [190]

	2		10		6		

(Hint: imagine a break such as a comma between 'walk' and 'back'.)

OLD WORKHORSES

These are the clichés of the game that are frequently used — confounding beginners and arousing an 'Oh, not again' response from veterans. If you're a beginner you'll soon join the ranks of the groaners. For the record, amongst the commonest are '**feller**' to denote something to do with the lumberjack trade, '**flower**', '**banker**' or '**runner**' to denote a river, and '**number**' to denote some kind of painkiller. Another one, which we might call '**The Hidden AND**', requires AND to be inserted, without a direct reference to it in the clue as in the following example:

Transport complete water supply with skill (8)

This is a compound clue where we have to build up components to satisfy the definition 'Transport'. The 'complete water supply' referred to is 'Hot and Cold' in its abbreviated form — H AND C. To this we add ART (i.e. 'skill') to get H-AND-C+ART, which we simply push together to get HANDCART.

But be aware that implied connecting words other than 'and' can be used. Bear this in mind with the following variation — which may be short but is quite difficult.

Thirteen letters? It's not much (4)   [023]

	7		8

(If you're stuck with this one, think how one might describe the first thirteen letters of the alphabet.)

THE PHANTOM WORD

Some clues will make reference to a word that does not figure in the clue or the answer at all — there is a phantom word lurking in the background. Usually it takes the form of telling us what the answer *would* become if we added a component to it. Example:

Not so much of that and get on for the instruction! (4)

The definition is 'not so much' and the answer is LESS. However, unlike other types of clue, we are not told *directly* how to get the answer. Instead we are told that once we have the answer, we can verify that it is right because if we add ON to it we would get an 'instruction', namely LESSON.

The 'phantom word' clue is a close cousin to the omission clue, being in fact a mirror image of it. This is demonstrated by its capability of being re-written as an omission clue. For example, the above could be re-written as:

Instruction without working is not so much (4)

(The answer again is LESS and, if you don't quite understand how this is arrived at, see 'working' in the glossary.)

Although the following 'phantom word' clue is short, it might present you with a challenge...

No longer taking over for the examination (4)   [275]

	2		12

SPOONERISMS

The Rev. W.A. Spooner of Oxford has long been credited (or discredited) with the slip in speech where initial sounds of words are transposed so as to form some ludicrous combination. The standard one which is trundled out is 'The Lord is a shoving leopard' for 'loving shepherd'. One may wonder whether he actually said it or it is just an interesting tale, nevertheless the so-called spoonerism makes an occasional appearance in crosswords. The instances can be quite convoluted but a straightforward example is demonstrated by:

Nosy enthusiast swapping lids one's used in the kitchen (6,3)

The 'nosy enthusiast' is PRYING FAN which, with 'lids' or initial letters transposed, becomes something 'used in the kitchen', namely FRYING PAN.

PALINDROMES

A palindrome is a word which is spelled the same whichever way you read it e.g. LEVEL, ANNA. When the answer we are looking for is a palindrome we will be given an indicator such as 'in both directions', 'reflect', 'works both ways' etc. In the following, 'identifiable from either side' plays the role of a palindrome indicator:

Detecting equipment identifiable from either side (5)

which is satisfied by RADAR. Such words do crop up but, just as they are rare in reality, they are rare in crosswords too.

USING THE QUIRKS OF THE LANGUAGE — CONTRARY MEANINGS

The English language is a minefield of quirks and anomalies, and compilers exploit them to the full. We have already said that one of the characteristics of the language is that words can have several meanings, but in a handful cases the meanings are actually *contradictory* to each other. With these, the reader or listener can only know which meaning is intended by the context in which it is used. The classic one is 'cleave' which means either to split apart or to bring together — complete opposites to each other! Even the most educated person cannot give a meaning to 'cleave' without knowing the sentence in which it is used. (Similarly, in a technical context 'laminate' can mean either to split or to bond.)[1]

This specific kind of confusion is utilised in yet another classic of the language:

Having been behind, got ahead (9)

This plays on the fact that 'succeed' can mean either to go *behind* or to go in *front*! (One wonders what newcomers to the language think of such words.) Hence the answer to the above conundrum is SUCCEEDED.

This tendency in the language not only confuses foreigners but is also used by compilers to confuse anybody trying to do their cryptic crosswords. The following is an interesting variation, making use of the two conflicting meanings of the phrase 'on the level'.

On the level? Yes and no (8,2)   [004]

	7		6			9			10

ANOTHER QUIRK OF THE LANGUAGE — FIGURES OF SPEECH

The language is rich in figures of speech. For example, 'to pay cash on the nail' means to pay immediately in coin of the realm. On the quay in Bristol harbour one can still see a flat capstan called 'The Nail' on which the money for cargoes was paid and Bristolians claim that this is the origin of the term. This may be so, but in most cases the origins of figurative speech are lost in the mists of time. Either way, compilers will have fun presenting us with figures of speech in their literal form such as this one:

Deteriorate, having acquired mostly different setters? (2,2,3,4)   [139]

11		7			9		5		11	

[1] We could note that while such words have come about in a natural way, there is a development whereby words are given their opposite meanings deliberately. It seems to have originated long ago in the jazz world where 'bad' and 'wicked' came to mean 'good'. However, recent generations of young people (who may have no interest in jazz) have picked up the habit of using words to mean their opposite as part of the language of their youth culture. To date, I have only come across a few examples where this contrivance has been used in a crossword but it is so widespread 'on the street' that we should be prepared for increasing incidence in our puzzles.

FOREIGN WORDS & PHRASES

Short foreign words are very useful to compilers as components in building up words in compound clues. So these, especially definite and indefinite articles (*un, une, die, das, der, il*, etc.) turn up quite regularly. Invariably a conventional device will signal them, for example 'a French' cues UN — so 'a French article' can lead to UNIT (i.e. UN+IT). Similarly, 'the German South' cues DIES (i.e. DIE+S). A variation is to use a foreign locality as an indicator that we are to go beyond the borders of the English language. So 'one in Paris' cues UNE, 'one in Berlin' cues EIN and so on.

Beyond the short words being used as building blocks there are complete foreign words and phrases that have become naturalized and are in frequent use in English (*persona non grata, ad nauseam, au gratin* and the like). So do not be surprised when you are expected to supply these as answers in their own right.

And, in so doing, we must be mindful of our opponents' deviousness, for they have an assortment of tricks for disguising the fact they are after a foreign word or term. As with all these things we cannot be all-encompassing so let's consider one: Nice. When Nice is placed at the start of a sentence, the beginner can be forgiven for allowing themselves to be misdirected into thinking the only reason it has a capital letter is because it is at the beginning of a sentence. However, with a capital letter, Nice is also the name of a French town and thus can indicate covertly that something French is required. For example,

Nice words for leavers (2,6)

can send you off on a wild goose chase for nice words — until you recognise the ploy and come up with AU REVOIR.

ACROSS AND DOWN CLUES — A NOTE ON INDICATORS

Be wary that indicators can have different implications dependent on whether they are situated in ACROSS or DOWN clues. The common cases involve the ordering of letters. For example, as one normally writes and reads horizontally, the phrase 'to the left' in an ACROSS clue can be a *reversal* indicator. Popular equivalents in a DOWN clue are 'to the north' (i.e. going up) or 'rising' as in:

I don't believe it! The river, even, is rising (5) (DOWN)

The basis is R (i.e. 'river') + EVEN, which we reverse (as indicated by 'rising' in the Down clue) to get NEVER, an equivalent of 'I don't believe it!'.

The following uses the same indicator and is quite straightforward (provided you know a little geography).

Where the big lake is rising? (4) (DOWN) [244]

12		13	

But compilers can be quite ingenious in thinking up reversal indicators in 'Down' clues. Consider:

Game for an aircraft manoeuvre on taking off (4) (DOWN)

On the face of it, 'taking off' is not a reversal indicator. However, this is a DOWN clue, so the notion of 'taking off' (i.e. rising, going up) *is* quite legitimate as a reversal indicator. The particular 'aircraft manoeuvre' is LOOP which we reverse to give us POOL, the 'game' in question.

LINKED CLUES

The clues in a newspaper grid can be linked in several ways. For example, on a day marked by some anniversary or religious festival, several clues may reflect the theme. You may be advised of this or *left to discover it for yourself*. More often, clues are linked in pairs. This is done in one of two ways. Firstly, a clue can draw on another for components, e.g. 'the first of 3' can call for the first letter of clue no. 3 to be used. There are several permutations of this kind of link such as the answer of one clue being an anagram of the answer to another. Most commonly, consecutive clues will be linked by a series of dots, as in:

1 One English poet's bashful about Parisenne ... (7)

2 ... while another's in her bed endlessly (7)

'Bashful' is SHY and 'Parisienne' is ELLE (French for 'she') so the answer to (1) is SH(ELLE)Y = SHELLEY, the poet. The two series of dots have helpfully told us that both answers are poets. In (2) we omit the last letter of BERTH ('bed') to get HER + BERT = HERBERT, another poet. However, beware. Just as often, the setter will use a *false* connection between consecutive clues as a form of misdirection. Witness the following:

1 Control grave's first inscription ... (4)

2 ... graven data reinterpreted for a modern audience (5-5)

RIP is the 'inscription' referred to in (1) leading to G + RIP = GRIP, i.e. 'control'. The second is solved as an anagram leading to AVANT GARDE. As you can see, there is *no* connection between them and the setter has mischievously used the placing of two similar words (grave/graven) in the two clues to suggest there is a link.

THE SCENARIO

We have defined the *scenario* as the theme running through the clue that provokes a certain image. The following is a clue which presents us with a scenario in keeping with the answer and so is helpful.

Messenger, possibly, one restricted by awkward kerb? (5)

This is a nesting type clue with 'messenger' as the definition. 'Restricted' is the nesting indicator while 'awkward' is an anagram indicator, the result of which is that we simply have to nest I ('one') within an anagram of KERB. When we achieve the answer BIKER we might pause and admire the skill with which the whole clue has been kept to one theme.

However, we have also mentioned in passing that the scenario is just as likely to have been devised to mislead. Consider the following admirably written clue.

Read Van Gogh's last letter arranging for a gallery (8)

We have three items in the clue, which hang neatly together. 'Van Gogh' and 'gallery' embody the notion of painting. Another nice touch is that Van Gogh was known for writing letters, particularly to his brother. However, this erudite knowledge is of no use to us at all — because the answer has nothing to do with art! The target word is 'gallery' and 'arranging' signals an anagram. Hence, the answer is arrived at through an anagram of READ VAN + H (i.e. 'Gogh's last letter') giving us VERANDAH, a form of gallery!

The following is another well-constructed clue that also presents a scenario that has little to do with the answer. So beware — it has nothing to do with chess. You have been warned!

Allow bishop and another piece to be taken (5)   [301]

1			3	

FINALLY: DOWN THE RABBIT-HOLE — WHERE THE CROSSWORD IS IN A LITTLE WORLD OF ITS OWN

It is fitting to end our analysis of cracking the code in crosswords by looking at the kind of clue which refers to the crossword game itself. With this ploy, the clue only has meaning within its own terms of reference. In other words, we have gone down Alice's rabbit-hole to a world where the rules of logic are different. A good example of this is the following.

Edit clueing device to cope with temporary problem (4,4)

We have learned that normally we can approach a clue in one of two ways:

1. We can either construct the answer from the instructions, using the indicators and components; or

2. We can identify the definition and consider various synonyms until we have something appropriate, hopefully the answer. In other words, we can work backwards.

However, in the above example the construction method is virtually debarred to us because the 'clueing device' is referring to a specific crossword indicator but we are not given any hint of which one! So, it is probably wisest only to consider tackling such a clue when you already have a few checked letters in.

Failing having no letters entered, you have to try to identify the definition. On the face of it, it looks like it could be 'edit' or 'temporary problem'. In fact, the definition is 'cope with temporary problem'. What the compiler has done is reverse the game. He has given you the 'answer' and *you* have to provide the clue! In other words, what do you have to do to TIDE (in crossword lingo) to get EDIT? Answer: TIDE OVER — which matches the definition, 'cope with temporary problem'.

And finally, one for you in this topsy-turvy vein:

Selur? (7,3,5)   [226]

1			5		2		7		12	13		4	12	

Checked letters for this chapter

1	2	3	4	5	6	7	8	9	10	11	12	13
B	N	O	L	D	A	T	M	H	P	G	E	R

Chapter 9

CONCLUSION

We have now given you all the basics we can think of for tackling cryptic crosswords. However, you can only develop skill in solving puzzles — and appreciate the enjoyment that it brings — by constant practice. And you can begin your practice *immediately* by working through the clues which now follow. So let us summarise the main points.

1. Remember that in the majority of cases the definition or synonym for the answer is the *first* or *last* part of the clue.

2. Ignore the obvious. Remember that the setter is *always* trying to trap you with the obvious, so think laterally; look for a *less* obvious meaning.

3. Consider each word *separately*, especially when the words have been made to look as if they go together. Also, by implication, consider words *together* when they have been made to look as though they are separate.

4. Remember that the basis for crosswords is a set of *codes* and there are two lots. *Firstly*, those that refer to words and components, and we have already come across many. ('Expert' usually calls for ACE, 'depressed' can call for LOW, 'record' usually means LOG, EP, CD, LP and so on.) *Secondly*, there are those code words and phrases that serve as indicators to the tricks that the compiler is playing — anagrams, homophones, nesting and so on. And bear in mind that compilers are an ingenious lot and are forever devising new tricks with which to challenge us.

5. Regularly having a go with a daily paper, even if you don't do too well to start with, is not only the best way because 'practice makes perfect' but also because one of the secrets of crossword-solving is to get into the mind of a particular newspaper's compiler (or team of compilers). Compilers really do differ in their habits, conventions, preferences and assorted quirks.

6. Finally, when you are stuck with a particular grid, don't just give up. Lay it aside for a while, do something else and return to it at another convenient time.

So, if you are a beginner and a perseverer, this book should already be helping you to make inroads into grids. And, if it's doing that for you, it's done its job. OK, keep your wits about you, be alert to the continual flood of new words and, if this is your copy, don't be afraid to write your own discoveries in the margins — that's what they're there for.

We hope that you not only learn from but also enjoy the practice clues that we have selected from a wide range of newspapers and magazines now coming up. So, to beginners and veterans alike — happy puzzling!

PRACTICE CLUES

A. PRACTICE CLUES BASED ON TYPE OF CLUE

From now on you're on your own but in this section you will at least know what trick to look out for. The following clues have been carefully selected, not only for their quality but also to make a particular point. With the hints provided and some thought, we hope that you will be able to solve most of them. The codes will be found in the glossary. However, if you can't answer a specific clue and eventually have to look up the answer, you will benefit by spending a little time working out how the clue works — what is its logic? what is the definition in the clue? what indicators are being used?

THE RUN

The following are uncomplicated runs — with no other trickery to be worried about.

Animal shut in hovel kicks (3) [143]

Hobo lustily grabs Greek coin (6) [019]

Outward appearances of a cad, esteemed to some extent (7) [024]

There's some originality in oil platform (3) [121]

Dines in style at smart restaurants (4) [022]

Dim nincompoop a questionnaire will expose (6) [159]

She's in a fine state (5) [065]

Consequently what husbands conceal (4) [305]

To some extent, a popular choice — for arboriculturalists? (5) [142]

Test of morality (4) [096]

ANAGRAMS

From this point on you will be given the option of using checked letters but remember it will be better practice if you have a real think first.

Pays out, but not in silence apparently (4) [038]

		1	

Was angry getting a bad grade (5) [062]

4			2	

Complain of poor table (5) [033]

	6		7	

Cater for change just a bit (5) [105]

	4		9	

Eeyore's upset by blemish (7) [025]

		2		3		2

Start writing notes out (5) [160]

	5		2	

Maybe kills for the ability (5) [086]

		8	6	

State upheaval just a sample (5) [017]

10				2

Halpern's exploded into little bits (8) [050]

11		4			5		6

Somehow reproduce sequence of actions (9) [148]

1			9				4	

Lamenting broken pact (9) [079]

	6			5		2		10

Minor misbehaving with this artisan (9) [306]

8		3		11			10	

Checked letters for ANAGRAMS

1	2	3	4	5	6	7	8	9	10	11
P	E	O	R	N	L	A	I	C	T	S

HOMOPHONES

Regretted sounding impolite? (4)   [312]

	1	5	

Bitterness voiced in private (7)   [165]

2			3		1	

Cuts in twos, we hear (5)   [241]

	4		5	

Class is shy in audition (5)   [248]

3		6		5

Times reporter's additional item on English rural region (6)   [028]

	7		8		2

Chimney wind indicator for the conceited, we hear (4)   [307]

		9	

Look bad-tempered, say (4)   [132]

	10		9

The clear sound of an aircraft (5)   [250]

11		4		9

Handled yacht soundly in rough (5)   [044]

3		1		

Money lent, we hear when single (4)   [120]

	8		5

Be the best letters to represent 40, we hear (5)   [150]

	7		5	

Herb in season, so to speak (5)   [239]

12				5

It sounds as if a shoe seems to laugh at a vice (8)   [217]

	8		3		6		9

In moments, quoted an example (8)   [290]

10		6		4		3	

Checked letters for HOMOPHONES

1	2	3	4	5	6	7	8	9	10	11	12
U	R	C	A	E	S	X	O	N	I	P	T

THE COMPOUND

You may remember that the solution of the compound clue is achieved by putting together components like a set of Lego bricks. In the following the number **before** each clue indicates how many components need to be used to build up the answer.

(TWO) Sailor posted as missing (6)
[029]

1		2			3

(TWO) It's complete in French flag (6)
[099]

4		3		5	

(THREE) Construct ring road on royal command (5)
[249]

	5		4	

(THREE) Start to complain about church being just a shell (5)
[308]

6			6	

(FOUR) Go in quietly, rebel and start secret projects (11)
[116]

4			4			5		2		2

(FIVE) What defines class, and orders levy on old motor yacht (8)
[052]

	1		7			8	

(FIVE) Get rid of former word, one name gradually destroyed (11)
[063]

4		3			8			1		4

(SIX) Lover of the past, I shoot back with weight about me on a file (14)
[218]

3		1			3		7		1			2	

(SIX) Bird (American) with man in charge of American play (5,10)
[134]

3				2			9			10		6		2

Checked letters for COMPOUND CLUES

1	2	3	4	5	6	7	8	9	10
A	S	T	E	R	C	O	M	D	N

NESTING
(for future use, note the nesting indicator being used in each case)

Thought I would have a cover point (4) [031]

	1		

In particular, the return from drinks containing ice (7) [294]

	4			5		6

Talk politics when a union leader's in a spot? (5) [219]

	4			7

It's a privilege to get on in time (6) [296]

	9		9		2

Flogged turf getting pound (4) [122]

10		6	

Bearing nothing about in the store (6) [262]

11			2		3

Taught to rule soundly, in Edward's case (7) [313]

	2			3		

Lazy student put in incomplete suggestion (4) [140]

	1		

Daring king caught by revolutionary quits (5) [048]

3		2		8

Are about to perform worship (5) [020]

	1		2	

A cleric angered about being questioned (7) [162]

2		1		6		1

Novice to include endless anger (4)[085]

7		2	

Inaccurate summary I am ultimately irate about (9) [080]

5		4		8			10	

Mere chance may cause a decrease in composure (11) [206]

10		2		3			4		7	

Checked letters for NESTING clues

1	2	3	4	5	6	7	8	9	10	11
D	R	N	P	I	L	T	E	O	S	B

REVERSALS
(for future reference note the reversal indicators)

Beat members up (5) [039]

	1		2	

Isn't up to 100 mph (3) [263]

1		

Got going again when the roofer returned (5) [055]

3		4		1

Make a mistake over students (4,2) [220]

	4		5		5

This game's up and it's a fiddle (5, Down) [179]

	2		1	

Gnome used to be retiring (3) [146]

		6

Duck boy's seen flying north east (5, Down) [314]

7		2		7

It makes a change from 'hands up!' (4, Down) [082]

	6		5

Rung up little darlings (4, Down) [225]

	1		5

Give out number when turning up punctually (2,4) [195]

	8			9	

Catch a number on the rebound (3) [302]

8		

Rep in setback, employees being short-term (5) [157]

1		9		

By ten to one got transport back: he's strict (8) [119]

9		3			8		1

Uneasy as always about its return (7) [208]

	7		1		10	

Checked letters for REVERSALS

1	2	3	4	5	6	7	8	9	10
T	A	R	L	P	W	E	N	M	V

STARTERS

(in the following the definition is at the **beginning** of the clue)

Bondsman not totally user-friendly (4)   [040]

	1		

Official getting Mary upset about nothing! (5)   [098]

	2			3

Those who take advantage with subtle ruses (5)   [209]

4				5

Chosen with love, being soft on Edward (5)   [127]

6		7		8

Carpet for Staffordshire university residence, reportedly? (8)   [213]

9		1			2		10

Logical nature of company woman in French church (9)   [221]

	6			3		11		

ENDERS

(in the following the definition is at the **end** of the clue)

Ruler lines to wear away (5)   [151]

1		6		1

Girl to accept ring soon (4)   [229]

2		6	

From galley, ten moved gracefully (9)   [035]

	10			2		7		

Two men but only one champion (6)   [315]

	2		3		11

Checked letters for STARTERS & ENDERS

1	2	3	4	5	6	7	8	9	10	11
E	A	R	U	S	O	T	D	K	L	N

MISCELLANEOUS LETTER INDICATORS

(for future reference, note the letter indicator and *how* they are used in each case)

First rule in being teased (3)   [032]

		1

Garment woman might put on baby's
head, one worthy of contempt (6)   [210]

1			4		

What is totally unacceptable in Central
Constabulary? (4)   [232]

2		1	

Think you can ring off? You only finish
up fighting (4,2)   [316]

	4		6		4

Leaders from Kremlin in Russia often
visited ballet (5)   [075]

	5		7	

Fish from front or stern of dinghy (4)   [203]

10		11	

Beethoven's Second encounters a
setback in favour (6)   [260]

		2			3

Performs ultimately in Gilbert and
Sullivan? (5)   [172]

	5		6	

'Unusual, futuristic and other-worldly'
starts to describe it (3)   [113]

		7

Reason open wound hurts you (3)   [284]

	8	

Prophet found with odd characters in
mail coach (5)   [240]

		9		8

Shock—initially calming legislation
unleashes mass panic! (5)   [130]

9			3	

What's put on kippers might be, oddly, worth eating (9)   [152]

		6		2				11

Checked letters for MISCELLANEOUS LETTER INDICATORS

1	2	3	4	5	6	7	8	9	10	11
B	T	M	U	I	G	O	H	C	D	R

B. PRACTICE CLUES BASED ON THEMES

The remainder of the book consists of practice clues based on popular themes in crosswords. All the tricks that we have discussed are employed in these but you will have no guide to what stunts are being pulled. However, you will have three things on your side: (1) the glossary (2) the usual option of putting in some checked letters, and (3) you will know that the answer has something to do with the theme of the section.

THE BIBLE

He who had everything (3)   [156]

		1

Biblical figure in the library (3)   [124]

	2	

Certainly not an expression of delight from a flood victim? (4)   [037]

3			

Performs part of the Bible? (4)   [135]

		1	

Biblical beginning (4)   [034]

	4		3

Five hundred keen to follow Biblical king (5)   [003]

	5		4	

Unruly crowd captures a kingdom of old (4)   [011]

	6		7

A mother for someone who didn't have one (4)   [180]

	4		

Victim of confusion losing head (4)   [026]

	7	8	

Lawman? Oxford detective's not right (5)   [128]

	6		8	

You may find it in the Bible if you will (9)   [059]

	8		1				3	

Checked letters for THE BIBLE

1	2	3	4	5	6	7	8
T	L	N	D	A	O	B	E

MEASURES

Measure the holes in the road (4)   [077]

	1		2	

Measure of motorbike drive? (5)   [222]

		3		4	

Sound unit to measure line by writer? (3) [041]

5		6

Early record holds measures of goods (5) [061]

7		3		8

Tin containing right quantity of fish (4) [101]

	9		10	

Name carried by old university church in Oz (5) [205]

1		10		

Work out the depth (6) [256]

	11				5

Farm vehicle loaded with a weight of rocks (5) [318]

12		9		

After December 1st you'll have to live with liberal measure of sound (7)   [094]

2		12				6

With poor coal, fire doesn't begin to give heat (7)   [212]

12		6			4	

Given some clash this could make ten of diamonds? (4,5)   [170]

5		3		8		11		7

A measure of a policeman's credit? (9)   [054]

	11		2			4	·	

Checked letters for MEASURES

1	2	3	4	5	6	7	8	9	10	11	12
O	D	H	I	M	L	E	S	R	N	A	C

FRIENDS AGAIN!

Friend's purchase securing 1000 in two instalments (5)   [068]

1			2	

Miserable attempt to go after mate (6)   [125]

	3		4		5

Foreign friend one's naming? No, all names withheld (5)   [169]

3			6	

Cockney pal not wanting a very large pair of trousers? (6)   [155]

		7		8	

Personal and popular note by friend (8)   [224]

7		4			3		

Associate following a pattern usually (8)   [002]

	8			3			5

Friend joining Home Office in bad odour getting excessive publicity (8)   [027]

1		9		5		8	

A US friend curtailed customary practice in sheikdom (3,5)   [097]

	1		2		3		7

One who recommends giving publicity to cave reconstruction (8)   [110]

	2		8		3		

Fellow at work almost icy having got the French disease (9)   [200]

10			9			6		

Checked letters for FRIENDS AGAIN

1	2	3	4	5	6	7	8	9	10
B	D	A	T	Y	G	I	O	L	C

MUSIC

Knock a style of music? (3) [245]

1		

Sunday school air (6) [117]

2		1		3	

Record a piece of music (4) [073]

4		5	

Stick in — continue innings (5) [184]

	6		7	

Perform song accompanied by piano (4) [230]

	8		

A piece of music that's pleasant to the ear (5) [006]

2		3		9

Boy going to start a ballad (4) [030]

	7		10

Musical intro to muffin? (4) [164]

1		10	

Sort of passage, big, modified, at one end (5) [084]

	6		10	

Music used to soothe baby (4) [045]

1	7		

Blow that for a cheap wedding ring (5,4) [277]

11			2		11			12	

Musical live wire (9) [092]

	7		12			5		1

Musical call to arms (5,3,4,3) [199]

6			3		10		5		7			10		4

Checked letters for MUSIC

1	2	3	4	5	6	7	8	9	10	11	12
R	S	I	N	T	A	O	L	E	G	B	D

ON FIRST NAME TERMS

He — a bishop! And embraced by a shady lady! (6) [076]

1		2			3

Backward chap accepts alternative for goddess (5) [046]

1		2		4

It will be the first of January before my boy appears! (6) [211]

	5			6	

Woman finds happiness with church? (5) [204]

	7		8	

I'm taken in by the lad! (5) [126]

4		6		

Johnny is an unconventional warden (6) [317]

9		1			

Gape at slim sound woman (6) [123]

5		3			10

Wife off to Paris? (5) [266]

	5			10

She finds herself with South America to the north (5) [231]

4				10

Lady from regiment with limited military group (European) (6) [223]

2		10			5

Nay, not him first! Odd fellow! (7) [064]

9				7		11

He's involved in social antics (4) [093]

	3		10	

Short lad scheduled to appear in first event? (5) [131]

4				5

Woman orders King's African Rifles first east, then north (5) [214]

	9			10

Checked letters for FIRST NAMES

1	2	3	4	5	6	7	8	9	10	11
D	R	L	S	E	M	O	C	A	N	Y

SHADY TYPES

Insulate a prisoner? (3) [047]

		1

Redhead, artist, four fellows and I mingled with the rabble (8) [246]

			5		6		5

Person that's disliked is soon sad, unfortunately (2-3-2) [278]

			4		7	

Cruel ruler, incredibly ratty going round North (6) [051]

		3		4	

A traitor in the fraternity (3) [137]

3		

Criminal intended to limit one's credit (9) [100]

2				3			4	

Politicians imposed on one - the devils! (4) [171]

	2		7

First tackle then hold hooligan (4) [303]

			1

He got South American sunburn (from excess heat!) (5) [118]

	6		6	

Cleaner retains meat for thief (9) [090]

	8	9			4		3

Snake's place? (2,3,5) [238]

	4	10			1			7	

Grown-up is not faithful to a couple of unaspirated girls (9) [304]

		8		10				3

Cheeky fellow the sailor's embracing a primate (10) [049]

11			12		4				7

Checked letters for SHADY TYPES

1	2	3	4	5	6	7	8	9	10	11	12
G	M	R	N	F	A	S	U	L	T	J	K

ASTRONOMY

Sky altar (3) [056]

	1	

A pair together being extremely silly, zany and giddy (6) [247]

		2		3	

Mars perhaps aircraft before end of flight (6) [254]

	4			5	

Austria initially gets backing from German star (4) [279]

	6		

Hunter of stars? (5) [102]

	1		6	

Something heavenly for me in bed (5) [309]

	6		5	

Not all fear the space-traveller (5) [074]

	7		8	

No order in revolving satellite (4) [107]

		6	

Note girl taking the lead's star-like qualities (8) [264]

9			4		7		5

One getting unto a star, maybe? (9) [147]

	9			6				8

Comic pilot Dan Dare's end as a space traveller (9) [095]

	4		10		8			11

Star returned good service in group practice (10) [141]

12		8			3			9	

Checked letters for ASTRONOMY

1	2	3	4	5	6	7	8	9	10	11	12
R	Z	G	L	E	O	A	T	S	N	D	B

Turn right over before reaching the tree rubbish! (5) [181]

	1		2	

Nonsense from the detective I hired? (2,3) [251]

3				4

Journey to Europe will be worthless (5) [153]

5				4

Females coming into a fortune? What nonsense (6) [069]

		6			4

It's what you'd expect to see in some old dump (7) [163]

1			7		2	

Cobblers show approval of gin (8) [282]

		8		5		8	

Bull only tethered at first beside private river (5-3) [202]

5			3				5

French refusal to feel is foolishness (8) [191]

		9		4		2	

Still responsible for such silly talk? (9) [233]

3			9				9	

Smart appearance after losing one's hair? That's silly talk! (10) [168]

7				4			8		

Checked letters for A LOAD OF OLD ...

1	2	3	4	5	6	7	8	9
R	S	M	E	T	F	B	A	N

Please note that the exercises on pages 102 to 109 are **new** to the 2nd edition. When you've had a go at them you can check them in the usual way. But the glossary, compiled exclusively for the 1st edition, may not help with all the clues on these pages.

CREEPY CRAWLIES

Wanting to have an insect? (3) [406]

	1	

Bug in religious splinter group (6) [361]

	1				2

Parasite turning over a new leaf (4) [325]

	3		

Jam I'd get would contain insect (5) [390]

		4		5

Snap back — get insect! (4) [380]

	1		6

Seemingly it prays and preys (6) [399]

	7		6		

Developing stages of young dog with touches of affection and enthusiasm (5) [371]

8			7	

Despicable fellow the underworld finds a worm (6) [363]

	7		4		

Posh woman encounters common female insect (8) [321]

3		4				4	

Sailor and aunt upset over the French spider (9) [333]

6			7			3	

Pull a stone out — find an insect (5-5) [349]

8		7			3				5

It may promise financial gain, or possibly deny promise (5,6) [355]

		1				8		4		

Checked letters for CREEPY CRAWLIES

1	2	3	4	5	6	7	8
N	T	L	D	E	T	A	P

AMERICANA

European hero of American novel (4) [385]

	1		2

Backed by the gun, seizing all the money (6) [378]

		3		4	

A present for the President (5) [404]

	5		2	

American Indian medicine man associated with bird (6) [341]

6				7	

States how man's clue could be revised (5,3) [392]

	2		3				6

Head of state was a follower of Calvin (8) [369]

	8		3		9		10

Do 'The Crab' on American pavement? (8) [352]

		9		7		3	

President and First Lady left in place of rest (9) [332]

5		8		10			3	

Outsiders in tough residential areas in America (3,6) [336]

11				11		11		

The President in *Casablanca*? (3,5,5) [329]

		10	7				11			8			10

Checked letters for AMERICANA

1	2	3	4	5	6	7	8	9	10	11
I	N	L	A	R	M	W	O	D	E	T

WINES

It's a new wine! (4) [374]

		1	

Slip during light drink (6) [345]

	2		3		4

Wine where one would expect water (4) [396]

5		3	

Drink one may have when the weather's inclement (5) [354]

6		7		8

To a girl, it's intoxicating (5) [402]

	9			4

Wine to make good parties! (6) [342]

	3			10	

Wine to plunder (4) [388]

		7	

Temporary accommodation for wine (4) [366]

		8	

Fortified wine, ruby — put order in (3,5) [338]

3					11		4

Must trainee soldier lose time in order to obtain drink? (8) [382]

6			7			10	

Spicy wine available in Capri shop (9) [357]

2		5		9		3		

A drink to provide a state of double trouble! (11) [327]

	6		8						11	

Checked letters for WINES

1	2	3	4	5	6	7	8	9	10	11
T	H	R	Y	P	M	C	N	O	E	D

BRITISH & NORSE MYTHOLOGY

Noisy god although a touch remorseful (4) [326]

	1		

Should he lose his master he'd still have his mate (5) [359]

2		3		

Some food in sacrifice to a god (4) [389]

	4		

Nothing rejected by stilted godlike figure (5) [368]

	5		6	

Fellow philosopher looking up love goddess (5, down) [400]

	7		8	

King for half a year and one short day (6) [384]

		7		1	

Goblin fish (5) [337]

		5		9

A good bar was sought after by the inhabitants of Camelot (5) [344]

3				9

Fairy may be hobbling about nothing (9) [394]

1			3			9		

Outlaw and thievin' criminal, reportedly (5,4) [353]

	5			10		5		

Sort of angry male making for wicked sorceress (6,2,3) [379]

2			3		10		6			8

She took Arthur's arm (4,2,3,4) [331]

9			8	5				1		9			6

Checked letters for BRITISH & NORSE MYTHOLOGY

1	2	3	4	5	6	7	8	9	10
H	M	G	D	O	E	R	Y	L	N

SEE YOU IN COURT!

Keep out of the company of lawyers (3) [334]

		1

Copes without start of grace for chief magistrates (5) [386]

2			3	

Twelve people spent half the month on the railway (4) [365]

			4

Before the beginning of the trial, turned state witness (6) [346]

	5			6	

Appearance money batsman doesn't want to lose (4) [393]

			7

Exasperated, listened to the evidence (5) [375]

5				2

Try to show sound sense? (4) [381]

	3		1

Size up the court evidence? (4) [339]

		6	

One who recommends giving publicity to cave reconstruction (8) [322]

	8		9			3	

Neat Tory turns out to be one legally empowered (8) [319]

	5			1			4

Order popular with union (10) [397]

	10			10		5			10

As a barrister might, carrying heavy luggage? (4,4,4) [362]

1			5		10		6			6	

Checked letters for SEE YOU IN COURT!

1	2	3	4	5	6	7	8	9	10
R	D	E	Y	T	S	L	V	C	N

THE BODY

When speaking, pull part of foot (3) [372]

	1	

A little lower, showing a bit of leg (4) [347]

		2	

Ship using joints? (4) [391]

		3	

Kind of jerk? (4) [358]

	4		5

It contains information before end of treatise (4) [343]

	5		5

I used teeth when coming up with a bone (5) [320]

6		7		

I cross in plastic, as they often bite (8) [350]

	4		8			9	

Drunk in Ireland, an exciting chemical (9) [332]

		9		4			8	

A protection, if I'd been taken in by a false premise (9) [364]

	3			5			8	

Contacted a motoring friend concerned with part of body (10) [351]

10		6					3		2

Part of body itches and one'll wriggle (8,6) [324]

		11		2		5		6		4			

Checked letters for THE BODY

1	2	3	4	5	6	7	8	9	10	11
O	L	P	N	E	T	B	I	R	M	H

107

THE ICING ON THE CAKE

Not much to eat? (6) [335]

	1			2	

A virtuous person eats small pudding (5) [373]

	3		4	

Father's irritating tea-time treats (8) [395]

5			6			4	

You'll hear I shout loudly for dessert (3-5) [348]

	7			1		8	

Secure provisions for return - cake? (10) [356]

9			6			9		1	

Something sweet could make a bee's lunch (7,3) [401]

7			2				9		

Sweet to serve at Oriental function (11) [367]

5	1				6		1		2	

If this is served at table, keep sweet! (6,7) [383]

7			6		4	5					10	

Dull person following a recipe instruction to make sweet (8,7) [328]

9		11		3				12		13			

Checked letters for THE ICING ON THE CAKE

1	2	3	4	5	6	7	8	9	10	11	12	13
R	L	W	E	P	T	C	A	B	N	K	U	D

MONSTERS

Monster is work in progress (4) [360]

	1		

Possibly fined the monster? (5) [376]

	2		3	

Robot has instruction to leave the spacecraft (5) [398]

1				4

Tease the fellow about being an object of terror (6) [407]

5			1		

Huge creature (a dog) returns to catch unknown evil (8) [340]

	6		7			8	

No good to knock out the head man outside; it will only bring forth the big fellow! (4,4) [387]

	2		1			3	

Creature existed to eat greedily (8) [405]

	9		9			8	

Are founts necessary to print vile creature's name? (9) [370]

3				9			10	

Bigfoot making Chas worried about illegal occupation (9) [403]

11			12			10		

A hundred and fifty honest sermons? Could be an illusion (4,4,7) [330]

	6			3		11		4			11		9	

Checked letters for MONSTERS

1	2	3	4	5	6	7	8	9	10	11	12
G	I	N	M	D	O	Z	L	E	T	S	Q

THE END!

The headless dog is dead (4)

		1	

[106] Final destination for the tramline going off-track? (8) [138]

		5			3	

Stop in and have food brought round (6) [276]

2		3		4

The designer redesigned it and finished! (8) [060]

		6		7		1	

The end of soft furnishings perhaps (8) [298]

		5		8		3	

'Fiendish, fiendish! Enough!' (8) [299]

2		3			4		

A valediction from a brave warrior, we hear (9) [083]

7				3		7		

Model has blemishes returning — that makes things unbearable (4,5) [194]

	8		9		9		8	

Checked letters for THE END!

1	2	3	4	5	6	7	8	9	10
E	F	N	H	R	S	G	A	T	C

AND FINALLY FROM YOURS TRULY...

Goodbye to port after brief rejoicing? (7) [236]

10		1		5		

001 SIDLE
002 NORMALLY
003 DAVID
004 STRAIGHT UP
005 LIKELY
006 SUITE
007 USE
008 LIMP
009 ABORTED
010 BALLOON
011 MOAB
012 PITCH INTO
013 AMPHORA
014 STOP
015 WALLOPER
016 TURN UP
017 TASTE
018 CRASH
019 OBOLUS
020 ADORE
021 GLEAM
022 EATS
023 ATOM
024 FACADES
025 EYESORE
026 ABEL
027 BALLYHOO
028 EXMOOR
029 ABSENT
030 SONG
031 IDEA
032 RIB
033 BLEAT
034 EDEN
035 ELEGANTLY
036 PEN
037 NOAH
038 YAPS
039 STRAP
040 SERF
041 MEL

042 ACE
043 VECTOR
044 CRUDE
045 ROCK
046 DORIS
047 LAG
048 NERVE
049 JACKANAPES
050 SHRAPNEL
051 TYRANT
052 TAXONOMY
053 STEALTH
054 YARDSTICK
055 RELIT
056 ARA
057 SOLAR PANEL
058 KILOCYCLE
059 TESTAMENT
060 RESIGNED
061 EPHAS
062 RAGED
063 EXTERMINATE
064 ANTHONY
065 NESTA
066 INKHORN
067 THREAT
068 BUDDY
069 PIFFLE
070 LEASED
071 CLUTCH
072 REPORTED
073 NOTE
074 EARTH
075 KIROV
076 DARRYL
077 ROOD
078 EGG-TIMER
079 ALIGNMENT
080 IMPRECISE
081 EDIFICE
082 SWAP

083 GOODNIGHT	124 ELI
084 LARGO	125 PALTRY
085 TIRO	126 SIMON
086 SKILL	127 OPTED
087 ROGER	128 MOSES
088 OVERT	129 KEYBOARD
089 PAUPER	130 CLUMP
090 PURLOINER	131 STEVE
091 LENIN	132 MIEN
092 CONDUCTOR	133 SELF-OPINIONATED
093 ALAN	134 TITUS ANDRONICUS
094 DECIBEL	135 ACTS
095 PLANETOID	136 SNORE
096 ORAL	137 RAT
097 ABU DHABI	138 TERMINAL
098 MAYOR	139 GO TO THE DOGS
099 ENTIRE	140 IDLE
100 MISCREANT	141 BETELGEUSE
101 CRAN	142 LARCH
102 ORION	143 ELK
103 ARCHER	144 NINEVEH
104 KNIT	145 UNSETTLING
105 TRACE	146 SAW
106 OVER	147 ASTRONAUT
107 MOON	148 PROCEDURE
108 RETCH	149 CHEATING
109 HALITOSIS	150 EXCEL
110 ADVOCATE	151 ERODE
111 LEAD	152 NIGHTWEAR
112 MANUFACTURED	153 TRIPE
113 UFO	154 DOUSE
114 ASSASSINATED	155 CHINOS
115 AGONY	156 LOT
116 ENTERPRISES	157 TEMPS
117 STRAIN	158 STEM
118 SATAN	159 OPAQUE
119 MARTINET	160 ONSET
120 LONE	161 DUNNOCK
121 RIG	162 RIDDLED
122 SOLD	163 RUBBISH
123 EILEEN	164 RAGA

165 RANCOUR
166 WALK ON AIR
167 SPOT
168 BALDERDASH
169 AMIGO
170 MOHS SCALE
171 IMPS
172 SINGS
173 EASE
174 REPEAT
175 ALI BABA
176 HARASSED
177 IMPORT
178 WINDOW
179 DARTS
180 ADAM
181 TRASH
182 STAGED
183 RUSH HOUR
184 BATON
185 CATO
186 PRIM
187 PLIMSOLL
188 TANGENT
189 PITTA
190 KNAPSACK
191 NONSENSE
192 NEAT
193 MACH
194 LAST STRAW
195 ON TIME
196 SLEIGHT
197 ILLS
198 VOGUE
199 ANNIE GET YOUR GUN
200 COLLEAGUE
201 VEND
202 TOMMY-ROT
203 DORY
204 JOYCE
205 OUNCE

206 SERENDIPITY
207 ELEMENTS
208 RESTIVE
209 USERS
210 BLOUSE
211 JEREMY
212 CALORIE
213 KEELHAUL
214 KAREN
215 WICKED
216 RAREST
217 MOCCASIN
218 TRADITIONALIST
219 SPOUT
220 SLIP UP
221 COHERENCE
222 CHAIN
223 RENATE
224 INTIMATE
225 STEP
226 BENDING THE RULES
227 JOHN THE BAPTIST
228 RANSOM
229 ANON
230 PLAY
231 SUSAN
232 TABU
233 MOONSHINE
234 HAIR-SPLITTING
235 PASSIVE
236 CHEERIO
237 RAINIER
238 IN THE GRASS
239 THYME
240 MICAH
241 PARES
242 EUSTON
243 HASTENS
244 EIRE
245 RAP
246 RIFFRAFF

247 SYZYGY
248 CASTE
249 ORDER
250 PLAIN
251 MY EYE
252 CORGI
253 EARTHLY
254 PLANET
255 STRICTLY
256 FATHOM
257 LEANT
258 SANITY
259 TARDILY
260 ESTEEM
261 RED
262 BARREN
263 TON
264 STELLATE
265 SWAM
266 HELEN
267 APPROPRIATE
268 CATER
269 SOLACES
270 BANK OF ENGLAND
271 PERIODIC
272 ROMP
273 LITHOLOGY
274 REPEALS
275 ONCE
276 FINISH
277 BRASS BAND
278 SO-AND-SO
279 NOVA
280 NEST
281 HEARS
282 CLAPTRAP
283 STRAP
284 WHY
285 RUMINANT
286 BASS
287 HEIR

288 ARRIVAL
289 AREA
290 INSTANCE
291 INGEST
292 FAST
293 SMOKE
294 SPECIAL
295 REHEAR
296 HONOUR
297 BLITHE
298 CURTAINS
299 FINISHED
300 EMENDED
301 BROOK
302 NET
303 THUG
304 ADULTERER
305 THUS
306 IRONSMITH
307 VANE
308 CONCH
309 COMET
310 ADVERSATIVE
311 CAMEL
312 RUED
313 TRAINED
314 EVADE
315 PATRON
316 KUNG FU
317 ANDREW
318 CARAT
319 ATTORNEY
320 TIBIA
321 LADYBIRD
322 ADVOCATE
323 ROOSEVELT
324 ACHILLES TENDON
325 FLEA
326 THOR
327 AMONTILLADO
328 BAKEWELL PUDDING
329 THE WHITE HOUSE

330 LOCH NESS MONSTER
331 LADY OF THE LAKE
332 ADRENALIN
333 TARANTULA
334 BAR
335 TRIFLE
336 THE STATES
337 TROLL
338 RED BIDDY
339 CASE
340 GODZILLA
341 MOHAWK
342 GRAVES
343 GENE
344 GRAIL
345 SHERRY
346 ATTEST
347 CALF
348 ICE-CREAM
349 PLANT-LOUSE
350 INCISORS
351 METACARPAL
352 SIDEWALK
353 ROBIN HOOD
354 MACON
355 MONEY SPIDER
356 BATTENBURG
357 HIPPOCRAS
358 KNEE
359 MAGOG
360 OGRE
361 INSECT
362 REST ONE'S CASE
363 CADDIS
364 EPIDERMIS
365 JURY
366 TENT
367 PROFITEROLE

368 WODEN
369 COOLIDGE
370 NOSFERATU
371 PUPAE
372 TOE
373 SWEET
374 ASTI
375 TRIED
376 FIEND
378 DOLLAR
379 MORGAN LE FAY
380 GNAT
381 HEAR
382 MUSCADET
383 CASTLE PUDDING
384 ARTHUR
385 FINN
386 DOGES
387 KING KONG
388 SACK
389 ODIN
390 MIDGE
391 HIPS
392 UNCLE SAM
393 BAIL
394 HOBGOBLIN
395 PASTRIES
396 PORT
397 INJUNCTION
398 GOLEM
399 MANTIS
400 FREYA
401 CHELSEA BUN
402 TOKAY
403 SASQUATCH
404 GRANT
405 WEREWOLF
406 ANT
407 DRAGON

GLOSSARY

The following is a list of code words commonly used in crosswords to signify indicators or components that are to be used in the construction of answers. The entries have been specifically selected to help with the clues in the present volume but you will find it of help for many clues in your everyday crosswording. For the source of the entries and a fuller version, see the *Pocket Crossword Dictionary* (published by Bloomsbury Publishing).

a, A ONE; PER; TOP; UPPER; be wary that 'A' is often used in the guise of being part of the grammar of the clue sentence when it is in fact a component to be used in constructing the answer

abandoned EX; FREE; LEFT; LOOSE; OFF; QUIT; SHED; anagram indicator; omission indicator

about A; AROUND; ASTIR; C (i.e. circa); CA; ON; OVER; RE; UP; anagram indicator; reversal indicator; nesting indicator

additional item MORE; PS

again MORE; OVER; RE; anagram indicator; can indicate an element is to be repeated

aircraft CRATE; JET; MIG; PLANE

almost NEAR; NEARLY; NIGH; omission indicator, usually one letter from the end of a word

altered anagram indicator

alternative OR; OTHER; anagram indicator

always AY (Middle English); EER; EVER

America AM; STATES; US; USA

American A; AM; GI; YANK; US

anger BILE; FURY; GALL; HEAT; IRE; IRK; RAGE; RILE; WRATH

angered GALLED; HEATED; IRKED; RAGED; RILED

animal APE; ASS; CAMEL; CAT; CONY; DOG; KID; LION; MOOSE; PET; RAT; SOW; STAG; YAK

around C; CA; anagram indicator; nesting indicator; reversal indicator

artist DALI; HUNT; MONET; MUNCH; RA; TITIAN; TURNER

attempt BID; CRACK; GO; SHOT; SHY; TACKLE; TRY

back AFT; BET; END; HIND; REAR; SECOND; SPINE; STERN; reversal indicator; last letter indicator

backing AID; reversal indicator; element to be placed at end of word

bad odour BO; PONG

bad-tempered MEAN; TESTY

bed BUNK; COT; COUCH; CRIB; DIVAN; FORM; KIP; LITTER; PATCH; PLOT; REST

before ANTE; ERE; PRE; preceding indicator

best BEAT; CAP; CREAM; DEFEAT; ELITE; FLOWER; PASTE; PEAK; PICK; PLUM; TOP; TOPS

big HUGE; LARGE; OS; TALL; VAST

bird CAPON; CHAT; CHOUGH; COCK; COOT; CROW; DIVER; DRAKE; DUCK; EMU; FINCH; FOWL; GANNET; GOOSE; HEN; JAY; KITE; KNOT; LARK; LIFE; LORY; MINA; MOA; PEN; PIE; RAIL; RAVEN; REE; ROOK; ROOSTER; RUFF; SAKER; SCOTER; SHRIKE; SNIPE; SPARROW; STINT; STORK; SWALLOW; SWAN; TEAL; TERN; TIME; TIT; WREN [ROOST; WING]

bishop B; MAN; PIECE; RR

bit CRUMB; GRAIN; JOT; LITTLE; LUMP; MORSEL; ORT; PART; PIECE; PINCH; SCRAP; SHRED: SNAFFLE; TASTE; TRACE; run indicator; can indicate one or two letters to be used from the following word, usually from the beginning

bit of run indicator; can indicate one or two letters to be used from the following word, usually from the beginning

blemish DEFACE; FLAW; MARK; SCAR; SMEAR; STAIN; TAINT; WART

bog MARSH; MIRE; SWAMP

borders of can indicate first and last letters

boss HEAD; STUD

boy LAD; PAGE; SON; SONNY; can signal a proper name e.g. KEVIN, PETER; very often signals the diminutive of a proper name e.g. AL, ED, HERB, JOB, NICK, NED, PHIL, RICK; STAN, TED, TIM, VIC; *see man*

brave BOLD; CREE; DARING; DEFY; DOUGHTY; FACE; GOOD; GRITTY; STOUT

broadcast AIR; anagram indicator

broken BUST; anagram indicator

brought round nesting indicator

capital AI; GOOD; GREAT; HEAD; LEADING; MONEY; SUPER; initial letter indicator; can refer to a capital city: ADEN; LIMA; PARIS; RIGA; ROME

care CHARGE; MIND; TROUBLE

catch BAG; GET; NET; SNAG

challenger RIVAL

charge, in IC

chessman B; K; KING; KNIGHT; KT; N; P; PAWN; PIECE; Q; QUEEN; R; ROOK

china AMIGO; CH; COBBER; CROCKERY; FRIEND; MATE; MING; PAL; POT

China CATHAY

church ABBEY; CE; CH; MINSTER; ORATORY; RC

clean BATHE; DUST; GROOM; PREEN; PURE; SCRUB; SWEEP; WASH

clear FREE: NET; NETT; OPEN; LIMPID; LUCID; OVERT; PATENT; PLAIN; RID; SHEER; STARK; VAULT; WIPE; anagram indicator

cleared up anagram indicator

cleric CANON; DD; MINISTER; PARSON

coarse CRUDE; EARTHY; ROUGH

cockney usually the cue to drop initial 'h from a word, as "tough cockney" clues ARD "cockney lady" ER (i.e. 'er), "cockney man" IM (ie. 'im), etc

code LAW; MORSE

comic CHAPLIN; DANDY; DROLL; FOOL; anagram indicator

company ACTORS; CO; COY; CREW; FIRM; CONCERN; GROUP; HOST; ICI; PLC; REP (i.e. stage company); TWO; THREE; TROOP

component BIT; PART; UNIT

conceited VAIN

concerned with IN; ON; RE

confusion BABEL; FOG; MESS

contempt, one worthy of CAD; CUR; HEEL; LOUSE; RAT

continue LAST; RESUME; can indicate that a verb is required which is followed by ON to make another word or component e.g. ACT/ON, BAT/ON, GO/ON, FLAG/ON

crashed, CRASHING anagram indicator

credit CR; TICK

cunning ARCH; ART; FLY; GUILE; SHREWD; SLY; TRICKY; WILE; WILY

damaged anagram indicator

darling DEAR; LOVE; PET; SUGAR; TOOTSY

December 1st D; DECI

decline DIE; DOWN; DROOP; DROP; DWINDLE; EBB; FADE; FALL; FLAG; LAPSE; REFUSE; ROT; SAG; SET; SINK; WANE

decrease DIP; FALL

decrepit, seem DODDER

destroyed, gradually ATE

detective DI; DICK; DS; EYE; HOLMES; MARPLE; MORSE; PI; TEC

disease AGUE; GOUT; TB

dog BARKER; BITCH; BITER; CHOW; COCKER; CUR; FIDO; FOLLOW; HOUND; HUSKY; MUTT; PET; PLUTO; POM; POOCH; POODLE; PUG; PUP; REX; ROVER; SETTER; STRAY; TAG; TAIL; TRACK; TRAIL; YAPPER

dope ASS; CLOT; DRUG; GEN

drink ALE; BEER; BEVVY; BRANDY; BREW; BOTTLE; CHA; CHAR; CHASER; CIDER; COLA; CUP; DOUBLE; DOWN; DRAM; FLIP; GROG; HALF; HOCK; JAR; LAGER; LASSI; LAP; LIQUOR; MAIN; MALT; MEAD; MED; NIP; NOG; PEG; PERRY; PINT; POND; PORT; PORTER; POSSET; POTION; PUNCH; QUAFF; ROSE; RUM; SACK; SAKE; SEA; SHANDY; SHERRY; SHORT; SIP; SLING; SNIFTER; STOUT; SUP; TEA; TENT; TIPPLE; TOAST; TOPE; TOT; WALLOP; WATER; WINE

duke D; FIST

duty list ROTA

East E; can indicate a component is to be used reading from right to left (i.e. east to west)

Edward ED; NED; TED

encounter FACE; INCUR; MEET

end AIM; BACK; BOUND; CHECK; CLOSE; DEATH; DIE; EDGE; EXPIRE; FINIS; GOAL; LAST; STOP; TAIL; TIP; indicator of first or last letter(s)

endless, endlessly EVER; last letter(s) to be omitted

English E; ENG

everyone ALL; E; EACH

everything ALL; LOT; SUM; TOTAL

expert ABLE; ACE; BUFF; DAB; DEFT; MASTER: ONER; PRO

expression of delight AH

extremely MOST; ULTRA; VERY; FIRST and/or last letter indicator

farm vehicle CART

fast FIRM; LENT; NIPPY; PACY; SPEEDY; STUCK; CAN INDICATE SOMETHING TO DO WITH LENT, ASH WEDNESDAY

Father DA; DAD; FR; PA; POP; SIRE

favour BOON; GRACE; HELP; LIKE

feel GROPE; SENSE; TOUCH

fellow BOD; CHAP; CO (i.e. co- as in co-worker)); COVE; DON; F; GENT; GUY; MAN; MATE; PEER; can refer to a man's name, *see man*

fiddle BOW; CON; FIX; RIG; SCAM; SCRAPE; STRAD; TINKER; anagram indicator

fiendish EVIL; GRIM; anagram indicator

fifty L

file LINE; LIST; MARCH; RASP; ROW

fine AI1; DANDY; F; FAIR; GOOD; OK; OKAY; RIGHT; SHEER; THIN

finish CLOSE; END; KILL; STOP

first A; ALPHA; ARCH; I; IST; LEADING; ONE; PRIME; PROTO; TOP; initial letter(s) indicator; ordering indicator

flabby LIMP

flag COLOUR; DROOP; ENSIGN; FADE; FALTER; HAIL; IRIS; JACK; PAVE; PENNON; PIN; SAG; STANDARD; STREAMER; TAG; TIRE; WAVE; WILT; can indicate something to do with pavement

food BRAN; BREAD; BUN; CAKE; CHOP; CHOW; DIET; DISH; EGG; ENTREE; FARE; FISH; FODDER; GRUB; HAM; MEAL; MEAT; NOSH; PASTA; RICE; SCAMPI; STEAK; TABLE; TART; TOAST; TUCK; WAFFLE; *see meat*

fool ASS; CHUMP; CLOT; COD; DUMMY; DUNCE; DUPE; GIT; GOOSE; JESTER; KID; LOON; MUG; NERD; NIT; NOODLE; NUT; NUTTER; PRAT; PUDDING; SAP; SUCKER; TWERP; TWIT; can also mean a dessert

for PER; PRO; TO; can indicate that the definition follows

for example EG; SAY

former EX; LATE; ONCE; OLD; PAST

fortune BOMB; DOOM; LOT; LUCK; MINT;PILE

forty XL

found in anagram indicator; nesting indicator; run indicator

French, in DE; EN

French refusal NON

Frenchman FROG; M; RENE

friend ALLY; AMI; BUD; BUDDY; CHINA; CHUM; COCK; CRONY; MATE; PAL

front BOW; FACE; FACADE; FORE; HEAD; LEAD; PROW; SHOW; VAN; first letter/word indicator; preceding indicator; can indicate something to do with weather, meteorology

gape at EYE

German D; G; GER; HANS; HERR; HUN; VON

ghost SPECTRE; SPIRIT

gin TRAP

girl ADA; ANN; ANNA; AVA; BETH; CATHY; CHLOE; CLARE; CORA; DAM; DI; DAWN; DEE; DOLL; ELLA; EVA; EVE; GAL; GRACE; HER; IDA; IRENE; ISLA; IVY; JO; JOY; KATE; KITTY; LASS; LILY; LISA; LULU; MAE; MAI; MARY; MAUD; MAY; MILLIE; MISS; MOLL; MOLLIE; NELL; NORMA; PAM; PENNY; POLLY; RITA; ROSA; ROSE; RUTH; SAL; SOPHY; STELLA; SUE; TESS; TRU; UNA; VAL; VERA; VI; VIV; use of 'girl' usually signifies the name is shortened

give off, out EMIT

give, to can indicate that the definition follows

go in ENTER

good BON; FAIR; FINE; G; HIGH; OK; PI; PIOUS; RIGHT; can indicate some religious association as "good book" for Bible, "good man" for Saint, etc.

group BAND; BATCH; BEE; BLOC; BOARD; BODY; BRACKET; BUNCH; CASTE; CELL; CLASS; CLUSTER; FACTION; FORM; GANG; GENUS; GP; LOT; ORDER; PARTY; RING; SCHOOL; SECT; SET; SIDE; SORT; TRIBE; TRIO; TROOP; WING; as a run indicator can refer to a group of consecutive letters within the clue

gun ARM; COLT; GAT; ROD; STEN

gunmen RA

hair, losing one's BALD; BALDER

hand DEAL; DUMMY; E; EAST; GIVE; MAN; MEMBER; MITT; N; NORTH; PALM; PASS; PAW; S; SOUTH; W; WEST; WORKER

happiness BLISS; GLEE; JOY

headless first letter(s) to be omitted

hit BAT; BELT; BLOW; BUTT; BUTTED; CLUB; CUFF; LAM; PAT; RAP; SLAP; SLOG; SMASH; SMITE; SOCK; STRUCK; SUCCESS; WALLOP

hold BIND; GRIP; HAVE; HUG; KEEP; LOCK

holds HAS; nesting indicator

hole CELL; CORNER; CRATER; DEN; GORE; JAM; LAIR; MINE; O; PIT; POCK; PORT; SLOT; SPACE; SPOT; VOID

Home Office HO

horse ARAB; BAY; PINTO; PUNCH

I am I'M

I would I'D

icy COLD

idiot ASS; FOOL; NIT; NUT; TWIT

impolite RUDE

in HOME; LIT; TRENDY; nesting indicator; run indicator; can indicate that whatever follows is synonymous with the answer; remember like all small innocent looking words, in itself can be part of the answer as "element unknown in club" gives ZINC (i.e. Z-IN-C); used as a prefix can indicate NOT

incorrect, incorrectly anagram indicator

incredibly anagram indicator

initially initial letter(s) indicator; adjacent word or element to go to the front of the other element

inside run indicator; nesting indicator; can indicate a component is to be nested within side

insulate LAG

intended FIANCE; MEANT

isn't NOT

joke CRACK; GAG; JEST; PUN; QUIP

journey JAUNT; RIDE; SPIN; TOUR; TRIP

keen ACUTE; ARDENT; AVID; COLD; CRY; GREET; INTO; LAMENT; LOW (e.g. price); MAD; SHARP; can indicate something to do with mourning

King CARD; COLE; ER; GEORGE; GR; K; LEAR; MAN; OFFA; PIECE; R; REX; RULER; SAUL; VIP

knock BASH; BAT; HIT; INNINGS; PAT: PINK; RAP; TAP

lad BOY; SON; *see boy*

lake COMO; ERIE; L; LOCH; LOUGH; MERE; TARN

laugh HA; HOOT; MOCK; SCREAM; TITTER

lead, taking the HEADING; STARRING; WINNING; can indicate that one component goes in front of another

leader AGA; BOSS; DUCE; HEAD; KING; POPE; STAR; initial letter indicator; can indicate something to do with a newspaper's leading article

learner L; TIRO; TYRO

leave DEPART; DROP; DESERT; EXIT; GO; PART; QUIT; SPLIT; STRAND; RETIRE; WILL

left GONE; L; LABOUR; LORN; ODD; PORT; QUIT; RED; WENT; omission indicator; run indicator

levy RAISE; TAX

liberal L; LIB

line ANGLE; ARY (i.e. A RY); BAND; BARB; CAREER; CORD; DASH; EDGE; EM; EN; FILE; JOB; L; LEY; LIST; NOTE; OCHE; PAD; RANGE; RAY; ROPE; ROW; RY; SCORE; SHEET; STREAK; STRIPE; TACK; TIER; TRACK; TROPIC; VIEW

lines BAR; LL; ODE; ODES; POEM; R; RADII; RY; SONNET; TRACK; VERSE

little BIT; DASH; DROP; MINI; O; PETITE; PUNY; SHORT; SHRED; SLIGHT; SPOT; TAD; TRACE; WEE; WHIT; abbreviation indicator

live ABIDE; ARE; BE; DWELL; QUICK; RESIDE

long ACHE; ITCH; PANT; TALL

loop BIGHT, NOOSE; RING

love ADORE; DEAR; EROS; FANCY; LIKE; NIL; NOUGHT; O; PET; SEX; ZERO; *see darling*

man AL; ALEX; ART; B; BEN; BERT; BISHOP; BLOKE; BOD; CHAP; DAN; DAVE; DES; ED; ERIC; FELLOW; GENT; GREG; GUS; GUY; HAND; HANDLE; HE; HECTOR; HIM; HOMBRE; IAN; K; KAY; KING; KNIGHT; KT (knight in chess); LAD; LEN; LES; MALE; MIKE; MILES; N (knight in chess); NAT; NICK; NED; NEIL; P; PAT; PAWN;

PETER; PHIL; PIECE; Q; QUEEN; R; RAY; REG; ROGER; RON; ROOK; SID; STAFF; TED; TIM; VALET; *see fellow*

many BAGS; LOT; LOTS; MASS; MASSES; MUCH; MULTI; OODLES; POTS; can be used to signal a roman numeral for a large number, such as L, C, D, K etc

married M; MATED; SPLICED; WED

mate BRIDE; CHINA; COCK; CHUM; COBBER; GROOM; HEN; MUCKER; PAL; TOSH; can indicate something to do with chess

maybe anagram indicator

meat BARON; BEEF; FLESH; HAM; LAMB; LOIN; MINCE; MUTTON; OFFAL; PORK; RIB; RUMP; SPAM; STEAK; VEAL

member ARM; BRANCH; JOIST; LEG; LIMB; PART

military group NATO; TA

model COPY; DOLL; DUMMY; FORM; IDEAL;LAST (i.e. cobbler's); POSE; POSER; SIT; SITTER; T (i.e. from Ford model T); TOY; anagram indicator

modification, modified anagram indicator; can indicate that one letter has to be changed

mother DAM; MA; MATER; MUM

moved SENT; anagram indicator

music AIR; M; MUS; PIECE; POP; RAP; REGGAE; ROCK; STRAIN; SWING; TUNE

name CALL; CITE; DUB; HANDLE; N; QUOTE; STAR; TAG; TERM; TITLE; FIRST NAME; *see man, woman, boy, girl*

need LACK; MISS; WANT

new MINT; MODERN; N; NOVA; recent; anagram indicator; can indicate that RE is to be placed before a word as a prefix

North N; initial letter indicator (as "the northern" clues T); reversal indicator

not all SOME; run indicator

note A; B; BREVE; C; D; DO; DOH; E; F; FAH; FIVER; FLAT; G; LAH; LINE; ME; MEMO; MI; N; NATURAL; PS; RAY; RE; SEE; SHARP; SO; SOH; TE; TENNER; TI; can indicate something to do with music; can indicate something to do with money

nothing LOVE; NIL; NIX; NOUGHT; NOUT; NULL; O; ZERO

number AIR; C; D; EDITION; I; K; L; M; N; NO; PI; PIECE; PRIME; RANGE; SONG; SUM; TUNE; V; X; *see song*; can of course indicate the use of any arithmetic number but the following are commonly used as components: ONE, SEVEN, EIGHT, NINE, TEN; plus this is an old crossword warhorse, based on the fact that the unwary solver will overlook the secondary meaning of the word with a silent 'b', indicating a specific painkiller e.g. ETHER

nut ASS; BEAN; BUFF; HEAD; SNAP

oddly anagram indicator; indicator for odd numbered letters to be used as "croft oddly" clues COT

off-track anagram indicator

old AGED; ARCH; AGED; EX; FORMER; GREY; LATE; O; PAST; RUSTY; YORE

one A; ACE; AN; ANE (SCOTS); I; SINGLE; SOLE; UNIT

order BID; BIDDING; CH; DECREE; DEMAND; DO; EDICT; ENJOIN; FIAT; FILE; GARTER; LAW; OBE; OM; PO (i.e. postal order); RANGE; RULE; SET; SORT; TRIM; anagram indicator; an architectural order e.g. IONIC, DORIC

originally initial letter indicator; in conjunction with a homophone indicator can indicate a word with the sound of a word's initial letter as "originally thinking aloud" can clue TEA

others ETAL; REST

out ABSENT; GONE; OVER (i.e. no longer available); anagram indicator (as 'let out' cues an anagram of LET); nesting indicator; omission indicator; can refer to being absent, insensible, being asleep e.g. DREAM

pain ACHE; COLIC; GYP; STING; STITCH

partner ALLY; BUD; CONSORT; DATE; E (from bridge); LOVER; N; MATE; OPPO; PAL; PARD; S; W; can also refer to one of the partners in a specific partnership e.g. DUCK/DRAKE, STALLION/MARE, EMPEROR/EMPRESS

party BASH; CON; DO; LAB; LIB

past AFTER; AGO; EX; FORMER; GONE; LATE; OVER; PT

pattern CHECK; FORMAT; MODEL; NORM

perform ACT; DO; PLAY; SING

performing ON; anagram indicator

perhaps can indicate that we have been given an example and we should look for a general category e.g. "mother perhaps" calls for PARENT, "perhaps siamese" can call for CAT; can act as an accessory to a homophone indicator; can act as an acknowledgement that the compiler is stretching a point; anagram indicator

piano GRAND; P; QUIET; UPRIGHT

piece BIT; CHIP; CHUNK; FLAKE; ITEM; LUMP; MAN; MORSEL; PART; PATCH; PORTION; SHARD; SLAB; TAG; TUNE; *see chessman*

pipe CHANTER; FLUE; REED; TUBE

pleasant GOOD; NICE; SWEET; TREAT

point AIM; CAPE; E; END; GIST; HEAD; ISSUE; N; NESS; NODE; NUB; PEAK; PIN; PRONG; S; SPIKE; TINE; TIP; TRAIN; W

police, policemen BILL; COPS; GARDA; GUARD; LAW; MET; MPS; YARD

politician CON; LAB; LIB; MP; TORY

poor BAD; DISMAL; ILL; LAME; LOW; NEEDY; OFF; ROPEY; SHODDY; THIN; anagram indicator

popular IN; HOT; LAY; LIKED; MASS

port HOLE; L; LEFT; PT; SEA PORT, commonly RIO; also ACRE, ADEN, DEAL, DOVER, HULL, ORAN

pose ACT; PUT; SIT

poses anagram indicator

possibly anagram indicator; also can indicate that the general category of the example given is called for

posted SENT

pound BEAT; HIT; L; LB; LAM; NICKER; ONER; ONCER; PEN; QUID; RAM

pour LASH; RAIN; STREAM; TEEM

power AC; DC; ARM; CLOUT; LIVE (i.e. as in live cable); MIGHT; P; STEAM; SWAY; TEETH

practice DRILL; HABIT; PE; PT; USE; can indicate something to do with law or medicine

primate APE; MONKEY

prisoner CON; LAG; LIFER; POW

private GI; HIDDEN; INNER; OWN; RANKER; TOMMY

proclaimed homophone indicator

provide BRING; CATER; GIVE; LAYON (i.e. lay on); anagram indicator

provided GAVE; IF

publicity AD; ADVERT; HYPE; PLUG; FOSTER; PR; PUFF

purchase BUY; GRIP

quietly P; SH

quits EVEN; LEVEL; SQUARE

rebel CADE (insurgent during time of Henry VII); RISE

reconstructed, reconstruction anagram indicator

record ALBUM; ANNAL; BOOK; CAN; CARD; CD; DIARY; DISC; ENTER; ENTRY; EP; FILE; FORM; LIST; LP; LOG; MONO; NOTE; PLATTER; REC; ROLL; SINGLE; STAMP; TABLE; TALLY; TAPE; TRACE; TRACK

redesigned anagram indicator

redhead R

regiment RA; RE

rejoicing CHEER

rep AGENT; MP

reportedly homophone indicator

reverend REV; REVD

revised anagram indicator

revolutionary CHE; MAO; MARAT; RED; TROT; reversal indicator; anagram indicator

revolving SPINNING; TURNING; anagram indicator

riding establishment STUD

ring BELL; BUZZ; CALL; CHIME; CIRCLE; COIL; CYCLE; DIAL; DING; GANG; HOOP; INNER; KEEPER; LUTE; O; OUTER; PEAL; PHONE; ROUND; SET; TOLL; WASHER

river FLOW; R; a specific river name - common British examples: AIRE, AXE, CAM, DEE, EXE, FAL, FORTH, OUSE, SEVERN, SPEY, STOUR, TAFF, TAMAR, TAY, TEE, TEES, TEST, TRENT, WEAR, YARE; common foreign examples: DON, INDUS, NILE, ODER, PLATE, PO, RHINE, RHONE, URAL, VOLTA

road AI; AVE; DRIVE; LANE; M; MI; RD; ST; WAY

Roman RC; can indicate a Latin term or Roman numeral(s)

roofer TILER

round ABOUT; BALL; BOUT; BULLET; C; CANON; HEAT; LAP;

O; PLUMP; RING; SHOT; TURN; anagram indicator; nesting indicator; reversal indicator; can indicate something to do with drink or drinking places

royal R; REGIUS; can refer to a specific monarch, in full or abbreviated e.g. ER, GR

rule soundly RAIN

ruler ER; GR; KING; LORD; QUEEN; RAJA; REGENT; SULTAN; TSAR

rush DART; HARE; REED; RUN

Russian cash ROUBLE

sailor AB; HEARTY; JACK; OS; RATING; REEFER; SALT; SEAMAN; TAR; CAN INDICATE A FAMOUS SAILOR e.g. DRAKE, NELSON, ROSS

say AS; AVER; EG (for example); EXPRESS; MOUTH; OPINE; REMARK; SPEAK; STATE; TELL: UTTER; homophone indicator; or can indicate that the reference word is an example of the required word - for instance "left, say" can clue SIDE (note: for simplicity in the glossary we miss out 'SAY' where synonyms are examples)

school COACH; COED (i.e. CO-ED); ETON; FISH; HARROW; LYCEE; REPTON; STOVE; SCH; TEACH; TRAIN; TUTOR; can indicate something to do with fish

season FALL; LENT; SALT; SPRING; SUMMER; TEMPER; TIDE; TIME; WINTER

sensational success WOW

service ACE; FORCE; LET; MASS; NAVY; REFIT; RITE; RN; RAF; can indicate something to do with a church service, or a tea service

set EMBED; FACTION; GEL; GROUP; LAID; LAY; LOT; PLACE; PUT; TACKY; anagram indicator

setter DOG; I; ME

shady anagram indicator

shoot BAG; BUD; DART; FILM; FIRE; GUN; HUNT; PLUG; POT; SCION; SNAP; SPRIG; SPROUT; STEM; SUCKER; SWITCH; TEAR; anagram indicator

show approval CHEER; CLAP

show friendliness BEAM; SMILE

shy CAST; COY; LOB; RES; SHORT

side AIR; BANK; CLUB; EDGE; FACET; FLANK; L; LEFT; PART; PORT; R; RIGHT; SPIN; TEAM;VERGE; WING; also sides on a cricket ground: OFF, ON, LEG, etc.; can indicate one of the points of the compass

silly DAFT; INANE; SOFT; RASH; anagram indicator; with a whimsy indicator can indicate something to do with window (it has a sill!)

single I; LONE; ONE; ONLY; RUN; S; UNIT; UNWED

slim LEAN; SLENDER; THIN

smart appearance DASH

smart chap ALEC

soft LIMP; P; PLIANT; S; TENDER

some ANY; PART; PIECE; can indicate a word which means something less, e.g. NET; run indicator

song AIR; ANTHEM; ARIA; BALLAD; CHANT; DITTY; GLEE; LAY; LIED; PSALM; ROUND; TUNE

SORT ALIGN; ARRANGE; CLASS; KIDNEY; KIND; ORDER; TYPE; anagram indicator; can indicate a particular sort of person as "possessive sort" clues OWNER

sound AUDIO; BANG; BLIP; CHORD; CLANG; CLASH; DRONE; FIT; PING; PLUMB; PURR; RING; SANE; STRAIT (i.e. stretch of water); TICK; TICKING; TING; TONE; TRILL; WATER; WHINE; WISE; homophone indicator, as in 'by the sound of it'

sounding homophone indicator

South America SA

spinner TOP

spread BUTTER; RANCH; TED; anagram indicator

start BEGIN; ENTER; FLINCH; FOUND; JUMP; LAUNCH; OFF; ONSET; OPEN; SHY; TRIGGER; initial letter indicator

stick BAT; BATON; CANE; CLEAVE; CLING; CLUB; CUE; GLUE; GUM; JAM; LANCE; LEVER; PASTE; PIERCE; POLE; ROD; STAFF; STRING; TWIG; WAND; WEAR

stone AGATE; FLINT; GEM; HONE; LOGAN; MARBLE; PIP; PIT; RUBY; SEED

store BARN; DELI; HOARD; KEEP; RACK; RESERVE; SAVE; SHOP; SILO; STASH; STOCK

stranger ALIEN; ODDER; anagram indicator

strike BASH; BEAT; CLOCK; CUFF; DASH; DELETE; HIT; KNAP; KNOCK; LAM; LASH; LUNGE; PLUG; RAID; RAM; RAP; REACH;

SPEAR; TAP; WHACK; anagram indicator

student L; MEDIC; PUPIL; READER

subtle NICE; anagram indicator

suggestion CLUE; HINT; IDEA; THOUGHT; TIP

summary PRECIS; RESUME

sunburn TAN

Sunday S; SUN

superior A; ABOVE; ARCH; BEST; BETTER; ELDER; HIGH; OVER; PRIOR; TOP; U; UPPER; can indicate that one component should precede another; with capital letter can refer to the lake of the same name; reversal indicator

support AID; ARCH; BACK; BEAM; BEAR; BRA; BRACE; EASEL; ENDORSE: FAVOUR; FOOT; GUY; HAND; LEG; PIER; PIN; PROP; RACK; RAIL; REST; ROCK; ROOST; RUNG; SECOND; SIDE; SHORE; SLEEPER; SLING; SPINE; SPONSOR: STAGE; STAY; STEM; STRUT; TEE; TRESTLE; TRUSS; can indicate one element is to follow another; can indicate that an element is to be placed at the end

survey EYE; POLL; SEE; WATCH

swindle CON; DO; NOBBLE; RAMP; RICK; ROB; ROOK; SCAM; SKIN; STING

tavern BAR; INN; PUB

teeth, use your BITE; CHEW

terrible, terribly anagram indicator

thoughtless RASH

time AGE; AM; BIRD; DATE; DAY; ENEMY; EON; ERA; HOUR; MIN; MO; PERIOD; PM; SEASON; SEC;

TERM; TICK; YEAR; can indicate something to do with prison term

times X

tin CAN; PRESERVE; SN

tool AWL; AXE; BRACE; BIT; CLAMP; FILE; FORK; HAMMER; HATCHET; HOE; JIG; LATHE; PICK; PLANE; RASP; SAW

transport BEAR; BUS; CAR; CARRY; CART; DELIGHT; ENTRANCE; RY; SEND; SHIP; TRAIN; TRAM; TUBE

traveller FARER; HOBO; POLO; REP; TRAMP; TRIPPER

treat DRESS; STAND; USE

treatment CURE; DEAL; ECT; anagram indicator

tree ASH; ALDER; BAY; BEECH; BIRCH; BOX; ELDER; ELM; FIR; GUM; HOLLY; LARCH; LIME; OAK; PALM; PEAR; PINE; PLANE; POPLAR; SORB; TEAK; WILLOW; can indicate something to do with ancestors, lineage; can indicate something to do with SHOE

turf GRASS; LAW; SOD; SWARD

turned over reversal indicator; anagram indicator

two BI; BOTH; BRACE; COUPLE; DUET; DUO; II; PAIR; TWAIN

unaspirated initial H to be omitted

unaspirated girl, lady, woman ER

unconventional anagram indicator

unfortunately ALACK; ALAS; anagram indicator

unruly crowd MOB

unusual EXTRA; NOVEL; ODD; OUTRE; RARE; RUM; STRANGE; anagram indicator

up FAR; HIGH; OVER; RAISED; RIDING; RISEN; STANDING; UP; anagram indicator; reversal indicator; can indicate something to do with flying, pilot, trapeze artiste

upset RATTLE; RILE; TES (i.e. 'up' a reversal indicator for 'set'); reversal indicator; anagram indicator

used to be WAS; WERE

very little LEAST; WHIT

vessel ARK; BARQUE; BATH; BIN; BOAT; BOTTLE; BOWL; BRIG; CAN; CHURN; CRAFT; CROCK; CRUSE; CUP; EWER; FONT; FLUTE; GLASS; JAR; KETCH; KETTLE; LAUNCH; LINER; PAIL; PAN; POT; SHE; SHIP; SS; STEAMER; SUB; TIN; TUN; URN, VASE

vice GRIPPER; PORN; SIN

warrior BRAVE; FIGHTER; KNIGHT; *see soldier*

watch EYE; HUNTER; LO; SCAN

way AVE; HOW; RD; ROAD; ST

we hear homophone indicator

we're told homophone indicator

weight CT; GRAMME; KG; LB; MASS; OUNCE; OZ; PLUMB; ST; STONE; TON, TONNE

whip CAT; LASH; KNOUT; LEATHER; STEAL; TROUNCE

wine ASTI; CRU; HOCK; MEDOC; MUST; PLONK; PORT; RED; ROSE; SACK; SAKE; SOAVE; TENT; VIN; WHITE

woman ADA; AMY; ANGIE; ANNA; ANNE; ANNIE; AVA; CATH; CORA; DI; DOLL; DORA; EMMA; ENA; ENID; EVA; EVE; HEN; HER; HESTER; INA; JO; KAY; LADY; LASS; MAE; MEG; MO; MOLLY; NELL; NINA; PAM; RITA; RUTH; SHE; UNA; W; WENCH; *see girl*

woolly jumper EWE; LAMB; RAM; SHEEP; TUP

work GO; OP; SLAVE; TASK

worker ANT; BEE; HAND; TEMP

working ON; anagram indicator

writer AUTHOR; BARRIE; BIRO; DAHL; FLEMING; GIBBON; GREENE; MAILER; ME; NIB; PEN; POE; QUILL; SAKI; SCRIBE; STEIN; WELL

wrong ILL; SIN; TORT; anagram indicator